wedding plans
wedding crafts

organize · personalize · accessorize

CREATIVE
PUBLISHING
international
CHANHASSEN, MINNESOTA
www.creativepub.com

Copyright © 2003
Creative Publishing international, Inc.
18705 Lake Drive East
Chanhassen, Minnesota 55317
1-800-328-3895
www.creativepub.com
All rights reserved

President/CEO: Michael Eleftheriou
Vice President/Publisher: Linda Ball
Vice President/Retail Sales: Kevin Haas

WEDDING PLANS, WEDDING CRAFTS

Created by: The Editors of Creative Publishing international, Inc.

Executive Editor: Alison Brown Cerier
Managing Editor: Yen Le
Art Director: Megan Noller
Cover Designer: Barb Beshoar
Senior Editor: Linda Neubauer
Stylist: Joanne Wawra
Photographer: Tate Carlson
Production Manager: Helga Thielen

Copyright © Digital Vision photographs on pages 12, 16,
22/23, 26, 30, 34, 36, 46, 52, 57, and 59.

Copyright © Stockbyte photographs on pages 7, 8/9, 10, 15,
21, 24/25, 33, 38, 42, 44/45, 47, and 96/97.

ISBN 1-58923-130-9

Library of Congress Cataloging-in-Publication Data

Wedding plans, wedding crafts : organize, personalize, accessorize.
    p. cm.
    ISBN 1-58923-130-9 (soft cover)
    1. Handicraft. 2. Wedding decorations. 3. Weddings—Equipment and
supplies. 4. Weddings—Planning. I. Creative Publishing International.

    TT149 .W437 2003
    392.5--dc21
                            2003053099

Printed in Malaysia by:
 Tien Wah Press Sdn Bhd
10 9 8 7 6 5 4 3 2 1

Creative Publishing international, Inc. offers a variety of
how-to-books. For information write:
      Creative Publishing international, Inc.
        Subscriber Books
      18705 Lake Drive East
      Chanhassen, MN 55317

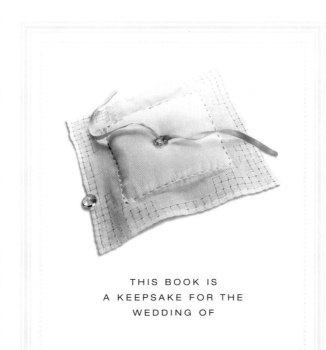

THIS BOOK IS
A KEEPSAKE FOR THE
WEDDING OF

_____

AND

_____

ON

_____

contents

introduction

YOU'RE ENGAGED! TAKE A MOMENT TO BASK IN THE EXCITEMENT AND congratulations and then get ready to get to work! Planning a wedding can be a daunting task, but it can also be a very joyful one. It is certainly an opportunity to learn a lot about each other and about the fine art of compromise.

Wedding Plans, Wedding Crafts has been created to help couples plan the wedding of their dreams. The first three sections in this book will help you arrange your priorities, set your goals, and make specific choices for your wedding day. Money-saving ideas and practical advice will help you watch your budget and avoid expensive pitfalls. Throughout the planning stages you will be referred often to the tools in the last section—worksheets, budget guidelines, timelines, calendars, and lists—pages that you will find essential as you interview service professionals, compile your guest list, manage your budget, and plan the details of your ceremony and reception. The wedding crafts section shows you 30 unique projects that will save you money while adding personal touches to your special day.

Ultimately this book will also serve as a keepsake. All the details of your wedding will be recorded here. In years to come you will look back through the pages and remember this time in your relationship when you managed to plan and pull off the most important celebration of your lives. You will have a permanent record of the special passages that were read during the ceremony, the songs that touched your hearts with their personal messages, every item on your reception menu, and which guest gave you the lovely crystal vase. A generation from now, you may look back at your budget and wonder how you got by so cheaply! Chances are, the receipts will still be tucked away in the pocket folders.

Sharpen your pencil and prepare for the wedding-planning whirlwind that is blowing your way. Put your dreams down on paper and enjoy the thrill of turning them into reality.

the big picture

YOU HAVE MADE A SIGNIFICANT DECISION FOR your life—to commit yourself to another in marriage. Soon enough you will be interviewing caterers, signing contracts, trying on gowns, and addressing invitations. But first you must look at the big picture and address the four Ws—when and where you will marry, what style of wedding to have, and whom you will ask to help put together and celebrate your wedding. Most likely you have already considered some of these things and dreamed of some possibilities. Once you have outlined the big picture of your wedding day, you will be better able to color in the details of your ceremony and reception.

when is the wedding?

THERE ARE 365 POSSIBLE DATES TO CONSIDER IN THE NEXT YEAR ALONE. How do you narrow them down? To begin with, even if you want a small, casual wedding with an intimate, at-home reception, you will need three months to get it organized. If you want a formal wedding with a large reception at a fancy hotel, give yourself a year.

If you are planning a destination wedding on a tropical island, you will likely find rates higher during the winter months.

TIME OF YEAR

The type of reception site you are looking for will affect your wedding date. The most popular reception sites are usually booked nine months to a year in advance. So in the beginning, you will need to be flexible by choosing perhaps one or two months during which you would like to get married and then narrowing your choices after you have inquired about the availability of your preferred sites. Before you book the date with a reception site, check also with your church or synagogue and officiant.

The most popular months for weddings are May to October, with June and September leading the list. Service providers and reception sites know they will be busy, so they often raise their rates during peak wedding season. If you can schedule your wedding between November and April, you may find more availability and lower rates. If you are planning a destination wedding on a tropical island, however, you will likely find rates higher during the winter months. During December you could be competing with company parties for reception sites, and many of your guests may have conflicting plans around the holidays. Some religions have restrictions against marrying during holy seasons, so be sure to check with your officiant.

Your wedding style and color priorities may point you toward certain times of the year. If you have always dreamed of a pastel wedding complete with tulips and daffodils, you should probably be looking at spring. If you want to dress your bridesmaids in rich jewel tones and carry a bouquet of burgundy mums, autumn seems the most appropriate time. Obviously an outdoor wedding should be held in a month when you can almost be guaranteed good weather, and that varies with different parts of the country. If you live in a northern climate and love the idea of a winter wonderland wedding, consider January or February but brace yourself for the possibility of too much of a good thing.

Other family commitments and celebrations can also come into play. May and early June are busy times for graduation receptions, so if you have close friends or relatives who will be involved with such celebrations, you might consider another month. Also be aware of any noteworthy anniversaries, birthdays, pending births, or planned vacations among the most important people on your guest list.

DAY OF THE WEEK

Weekends are by far the most popular days for weddings, when most people have a couple days off to travel, celebrate, and rest. Jewish weddings are not held on their Sabbath — between sundown on Friday and sundown on Saturday — and Christian weddings are usually not held on Sundays. Saturday night is the most popular time for wedding receptions, so sites and service providers book up quickly. If you can be flexible about the day of the week, you may find sites more available and often more affordable on a week night.

If many of your guests will be traveling quite a distance, or if you are planning a destination wedding, having the ceremony on a Thursday evening will give them time to enjoy the location for a few days before heading home.

TIME OF DAY

The type of reception you want to have and can afford to host will determine the time of day to hold the wedding. If the wedding is held during a span of time in which people would normally expect a meal, you should serve one. If your reception includes a dance, it is usually preceded by a buffet or sit-down dinner in the early evening. While this is the most popular arrangement, it is also the most expensive. You can cut costs by having a morning wedding, followed by champagne cocktails and brunch. Or you might prefer an early afternoon wedding followed by cocktails and hors d'oeuvres. Generally you don't want to leave more than an hour or two between your ceremony and reception, or you risk leaving guests with nothing to do. Just plan enough time for them to travel from the ceremony to the reception, if necessary, and allow for wedding photos if they will be taken after the ceremony.

what style will you follow?

LIKE THE CLOTHES YOU WEAR, THE CAR YOU DRIVE, AND THE FURNITURE that makes you comfortable, your wedding day should reflect your personal style. The perfect wedding needs to be perfect for you, not for your mother or your sister or your best friend, and certainly not for the fairy-tale model in the latest bridal fashions magazine.

Basically, there are three different styles of weddings: formal, semiformal, and informal. The location, time of day, size of the wedding party, and the number of guests determine the formality of the event. A wedding theme, also very dependent on location, is further developed by the colors you choose, the flowers and other decorations you select, and the menu served to your guests. The style and theme of your wedding will be expressed in every detail, from the invitations to the centerpieces to the thank-you notes.

> Generally you don't want to leave more than an hour or two between your ceremony and reception, or you risk leaving guests with nothing to do.

FORMAL STYLE

Invitations to a formal wedding are white or off-white with engraved lettering, and the guest list may include 200 or more. The ceremony, conducted by a member of the clergy, takes place in the late afternoon or evening in a house of worship or in a large, formal home or garden. The bride wears a white or ivory gown with a long train and veil. She has a maid or matron of honor and five to ten bridesmaids who wear floor-length gowns in formal fabrics. The groom and his attendants wear tailcoats. The evening reception, to which the guests wear formal attire, includes a sit-down or formal buffet dinner. If there is a dance, the music is provided by an orchestra or band. A limousine service transports the wedding party.

SEMIFORMAL STYLE

Invitations to a semiformal wedding need not be engraved. They might have a colorful element, such as a ribbon or sheer overlay that hints at the color theme of the wedding. The bride wears a long white or ivory gown with a short train and veil. The maid or matron of honor and two to six bridesmaids wear floor-length dresses in semiformal fabrics.

The groom and all of his attendants wear tuxedos or formal suits. Female guests wear fancy street-length dresses or cocktail dresses and the men can wear dark suits. The ceremony is conducted in the afternoon or evening by a member of the clergy and takes place in a house of worship, hotel, club, or someone's home or garden. The full-meal buffet or cocktail buffet reception is attended by 75 to 200 guests, and dance music is provided by a small band or DJ.

INFORMAL STYLE

Invitations to an informal wedding can be more creative and colorful, perhaps handwritten. The morning or afternoon ceremony may take place in a house of worship, small chapel, or someone's home or garden, and may be conducted by a religious or civil officiant. The bride wears a simple white or pastel floor-length gown, a dress in a less formal length, or a suit. The groom wears a suit or sport jacket and slacks. Each has one or two attendants who dress in a similar style to the bride and groom. The guest list is usually limited to 75 or fewer people. A breakfast, brunch, lunch, or hors d'oeuvres buffet reception may be held in a restaurant, in someone's home, or in a park, and guests dress to suit the location and time of day. Food can be catered or provided by family and friends. Background music can be provided by a single musician or a small band, or by recorded music on a home sound system.

PERSONAL THEME

Your color theme is set up mainly through the attire of the attendants and your choice of flowers. You can follow the scheme with ceremony programs on colored card stock, colored napkins or tablecloths, ribbon accents, colored candles, or table skirting. The personal theme of your wedding is expressed with elements of your favorite pastimes, music that sets a certain mood, readings that have special meaning for you, or flowers that symbolize your sentiments. Think about the interests that brought you together or that you now share. You can add personal touches to any style wedding with unique reception favors, themed decorations, and significant menu choices. Are you sports fans, nature lovers, classical musicians? Are balloons and confetti more your style than flowers and ribbons? Do you come from different ethnic backgrounds and want to combine the best of both worlds in a fabulous buffet? A wedding ceremony and celebration that carry your personal imprints will be meaningful and memorable for you and your guests.

where is the wedding?

LOCATION, LOCATION, LOCATION. NOTHING INFLUENCES THE STYLE AND theme of your wedding quite as much as where you stage the ceremony and reception. Whether you opt for the tradition and pageantry of a grand sanctuary or wander off the beaten path to a lakeside resort, the backdrop you choose sets the mood and enriches the ambience of your special day.

RELIGIOUS CEREMONY SITES

Most weddings, especially formal and semiformal ceremonies, are held in a house of worship. If one or both of you belong to a congregation and attend services regularly, you need simply contact the church or synagogue office for available dates and to see if the officiant of your choice will perform the ceremony. It's not quite that easy if you want to be wed in a church or synagogue where you are not a member or if you are of different faiths. Regulations, requirements, and fees vary greatly among religious organizations, so you will have to do some investigating. It is also possible to have a religious ceremony performed in a secular location, such as someone's home, a mountain lodge, or a public park. Select your officiant first and discuss your particular situation and desires with that person.

CIVIL CEREMONY SITES

Usually less formal, a civil ceremony can be held at city hall, in someone's home, or just about any place else the couple wants to be wed, provided the officiant of their choice is willing to travel there. Often, the civil ceremony and reception take place at the same site. The officiant for a civil ceremony could be a justice of the peace, a judge, a county or court clerk, a mayor, or even a notary public, as long as that person can legally perform the ceremony and sign the marriage license.

RECEPTION SITES

Have an estimated guest count when you shop for a reception site and select one that will accommodate everyone comfortably. You don't want to cram 200 guests into a tiny church basement, nor do you need a vast hall to entertain 50 family members and close friends. The site manager should be able to give you an idea of the room capacity. You may even be allowed to visit the site during setup for another reception to see how the tables can be arranged, where the dance floor is located, and where the bar will be set up. There should be room to set up separate centers of activity, like the buffet lines, a gift table, cake table, guest book, and punch table. Make sure that there are spaces within the site for all the activities you have planned: where your guests can gather to talk, share a cocktail, eat, and dance.

Hotels and conference centers that specialize in wedding receptions are likely to have ample electrical outlets for the band and any other electrical needs. They can probably provide you with microphones and a sound system for toasting, and they may even have a projector and screen available for presenting a photo montage, if you wish. Many locations provide and may require you to use their on-site catering and bar service, which can make your planning and shopping for service providers much easier. Such convenience could also be more expensive. Finding a caterer, baker, bar service, valet service, and rental company

Enhance your ceremony site by making an entrance door bouquet (above) or floral heart pew wreaths (below), pages 82 and 83.

are all things you may have to consider if you choose to hold your reception at a less conventional site, such as a historical home or a public garden.

Your desire for privacy should also be considered as you look for a reception site. Public gardens and parks and resorts are open to anyone, so if you choose to hold a reception there, be prepared to accept strangers as part of the décor. Even in large hotels, you are likely to share restrooms with the reception next door. If you are unsure about how much congestion this might cause, visit the site on the same night of the week as your own reception and notice if there are waiting lines or if the music from one room can be heard in another.

Look around at the room décor and decide if it will work well as a background to the wedding theme and style you are planning. Any carpet or draperies, artwork or statuary in the room should be subtle enough not to clash with your color scheme. If you are planning an indoor reception for early in the day, find a place that will let you take advantage of natural lighting. For a nighttime reception, make sure the lights can be adjusted to take full advantage of the romantic glow of candlelight without leaving your guests in the dark.

OUTDOOR VENUE

Ceremonies and receptions held outdoors often call for two sets of plans: the one you hope to follow and the one for inclement weather. The sunny, pleasant day you dream of may very well happen, but just in case it doesn't, you must have an alternate site reserved ahead of time. This could mean paying to rent a hall that is never used, if your guest list is long. For a smaller crowd, perhaps your parents' home can be on call. Tent rental is another option. In fact, tents today can be quite sophisticated, complete with dance floors, air conditioning, and all the amenities of home. Tents are a good idea even on a perfect day because they provide a place to keep the food and wedding cake out of the elements and a shady retreat for your guests.

If your outdoor wedding will be held on public property, such as a lakeside park or botanical garden, you will need to check with city officials to find out if any special permits are required for using the area. If your wedding will cause added street congestion, you may have to hire a traffic officer or arrange for a shuttle to a nearby parking facility.

To help you organize your thoughts and keep track of your options, interview forms for site selection and ceremony officiants are provided on pages 112 and 114. Make copies of the pages and take them to your interviews. When you have made your selections, fill in all the details on the final plan forms in the book for a permanent record.

Usually, expenses are shared by both sets of parents and the bride and groom, though how costs are divided is unique to every situation.

how will you make it happen?

BEFORE YOU GET TOO CARRIED AWAY WITH YOUR WEDDING PLANS, TAKE some time to set some realistic goals. Working out a budget may not be very romantic or inspiring, but it's the only way to determine what you really can afford and prioritize all your wedding wants.

WHO PAYS FOR WHAT

Once upon a time, the groom and his family paid for the rehearsal dinner, the marriage license, the officiant's fee, the groom's attire, and the bride's bouquet. That left the bride and her family picking up the tab for everything else. But then once upon a time, the bride lived with her parents until she was married and fewer women had meaningful careers.

More couples married when they were very young and wedding costs didn't run up to five digits. Today most men and women are self-sufficient and have been living on their own for a while before they get married. Sometimes the bride and groom foot the bill themselves. Usually, expenses are shared by both sets of parents and the bride and groom, though how costs are divided is unique to every situation.

Rather than assigning certain expenses to each of the parties, a more workable formula is to set a total budget by combining the amounts that each party is willing and able to contribute. Money is a touchy subject, but one that must be discussed at the very beginning before you make further plans. Each of you should talk with your parents privately to find out what they are willing to spend. Those amounts, along with your own contribution, will establish your target budget amount. Then fill in the budget on pages 108 to 111 to see how much you can spend in each area.

WAYS TO ECONOMIZE

Assuming the sky is not the limit, you will no doubt need to find ways to cut corners. That doesn't mean you can't have a formal wedding if you want one, but you need to decide which elements are most important to you.

cost-cutting ideas

- Your biggest expense is probably food, and that amount is dependent on the size of your guest list. You can either cut back on your guest list or plan your wedding for a time of day when you won't have to serve a full meal.

- Have your reception meal served buffet-style instead of hiring a wait staff. Talk to your caterer about other ways to economize.

- Have your wedding during a time of year, day of the week, or time of day when site and service providers' fees are lower.

- Search out a nontraditional site, such as a historical home, a public garden, or a zoo. Often the site fee is much lower than a hotel or convention center, even when you add the catering and rental costs.

- Make your own wedding veil (page 68). That alone can save you $200.

- Enlist the help of your attendants and other friends and relatives to help you make wedding favors, ceremony accents, and reception decorations, with the understanding that the sharing of their time and talent is part of their gift to you.

- Limit the number of attendants. Though you traditionally don't pay for their attire, you do pay for any flowers they carry, gifts for each of them, meals at the bridesmaids' luncheon, rehearsal dinner, and reception, and accommodations for those traveling from out-of-town.

- Make your own invitations, ceremony programs, and thank-you cards (pages 62 to 67).

- Alcohol is a big expense. Limit the open bar to the cocktail hour, or pay for beer and wine only.

- Comparison shop among vendors and service providers. When they offer package prices, make sure you really want everything that is included. Ask a lot of questions and look for hidden costs.

Try to make your decisions and extend your invitations to attendants soon after you have determined the wedding style and set the budget.

whom will you involve?

YOUR SPECIAL DAY WILL BE CELEBRATED WITH RELATIVES AND FRIENDS. Each of them, whether they stand beside you at the altar or attend as your guest, will witness your vows, pledge to support you in your marriage, and toast to your happiness.

SELECTING YOUR ATTENDANTS

The size and formality of your wedding determine, in part, how many attendants you will have. You may have as few as two (a maid of honor and a best man) or as many as you like. Usually there are equal numbers of bridesmaids and groomsmen, though that is also a personal decision. It's your wedding and you are free to mix it up a bit, even if that means the best man is really a woman and the bride's brother is her honor attendant. Try to make your decisions and extend your invitations to attendants soon after you have determined the wedding style and set the budget.

The attendants' roles include both personal and financial responsibilities. Besides paying for their own attire, your honor attendants will be your closest advisors, helping with planning, hosting a bridal shower, hosting a bachelor or bachelorette party, and taking care of special duties on the wedding day. Your bridesmaids will help with some of the planning and preparation, pay for their own attire and arrange fittings, attend bridal showers, pay for their own salon services on the day of the wedding, and also give you shower and wedding gifts. The groomsmen pay for their own attire and take care of wedding day duties. Make sure that you convey these responsibilities when you extend the invitations to your attendants. If someone you ask does not feel they can afford the time or money involved, they have the option to politely decline. However, if you are aware that being your attendant will cause financial strain for someone you dearly want in your wedding, you can make private arrangements to help them pay for part of the expense. Detailed lists of the possible duties and financial responsibilities of your attendants are on pages 138 to 140. Use these lists as a friendly reminder to them as the wedding day approaches and as a planning guide to make sure you have all your bases covered.

If you include children in the list of attendants, try to select relatives or close friends between the ages of three and seven for the flower girl and ring bearer. Girls between the ages of nine and sixteen can serve as junior bridesmaids. The flower girl might carry a basket or ball of flowers or, if allowed by the ceremony site, strew flower petals down the aisle. The ring bearer usually carries the rings (often imitations) tied to a small pillow or in an ornate box. Parents of child attendants pay for their attire and bring them to the rehearsal.

MANY ROLES TO FILL

If you have difficulty trimming down the list of people you wish to include in your wedding party, remember there are many other roles that need to be filled. The list at left describes the roles of other important wedding helpers.

THE GUEST LIST

Once you have set your budget, it is time to make a guest list. Knowing that the number of people who attend greatly affects the total cost of the wedding, you can either make the list first and then decide on the kind of wedding you can afford or decide on the reception site and wedding style and create your guest list accordingly. Diplomatically allot a number of guests for the bride's parents, the groom's parents, and each other. Don't forget to include in the count yourselves, your parents, your attendants, and the officiant and spouse. It is helpful for each side and the bride and groom to prioritize their lists, arranging names in categories of importance: immediate family members, extended family members, close friends and neighbors, and business associates. This will make it easier to select the people you must invite (the A list) and those you would like to invite (the B list). It is not always possible to divide lists equally, but the lines should be drawn within the same categories of importance. If guests on the A list send their regrets early, you can send invitations to guests on the B list within four weeks of the wedding. No one needs to know which list they are on.

Make a decision ahead of time whether or not to include children at the reception. If you decide against children, simply leave their names off the invitations. It is proper etiquette to include partners of invited guests if they are married, engaged, or living together, whether you know them or not. It is a nice gesture, though not an obligation, to invite other single guests to bring a date.

Keep a record of your invited guests on pages 130 to 135. Add names from the B list as invitations are sent. As you receive responses, record the number of guests who will be attending in the spaces provided. This will provide you with an accurate count for the caterer. Also keep track of gifts received and thank-you notes sent.

wedding helpers

- **PERSONAL ATTENDANT** There are so many details that need attention on the wedding day, the bride, her mother, and her maid of honor just can't handle them all. The bride needs a trusted, mature, organized, "take charge" kind of person to "sweat the small stuff" for her. In many ways your personal attendant can be your wedding day coordinator. A list of her possible duties is on page 139.

- **USHERS** Sometimes the groomsmen help in this role, handing out ceremony programs and leading guests to their seats. As a general rule, you should have one usher for every 50 guests.

- **CEREMONY PARTICIPANTS** As you plan your ceremony, you may find that you need readers, musicians, vocalists, cantors, altar assistants, acolytes, or others. Special friends and relatives who fill these roles add personal meaning to your wedding.

- **RECEPTION PARTICIPANTS** You may need someone to attend the guest book, two or three people to attend the gift table, perhaps an honored couple to greet and assist your guests as they arrive at the reception before you.

- **CRAFTERS** If you are lucky enough to have a few friends and relatives who are pretty handy, you might ask some of them to sew or craft items for the wedding as their gift to you. Things like your headpiece and veil, the ring bearer pillow, or a unity candle become cherished keepsakes when they have been handmade by someone who loves you.

invitations

INVITATIONS GIVE YOUR GUESTS A PREVIEW OF THE style and theme of your wedding. While furnishing the who, what, where, and when details, they also indicate the formality of the wedding by their size, color, type face, and wording style.

INVITATION ETIQUETTE

Formal invitations are white or ivory $5\frac{1}{2}$" × $7\frac{1}{2}$" single or folded cards sent in two envelopes with other necessary enclosures. The message is written in third person wording style with black engraved lettering in an antique Roman or similar font style. Semiformal and informal invitations can be various dimensions and may hint at the color theme of the wedding with a ribbon flourish, colorful sheer overlay, or the color of the card itself. They can be written in second or first person style, depending on how casual you want them to be. For very casual weddings, the invitations may even be handwritten letters on pretty paper.

　　Along with the formality of the wedding, the exact wording on the invitation depends on who is actually hosting the wedding and on the marriage status of the parents. Examples are given opposite for various situations; others can be found on Internet sites and in etiquette books.

Create semiformal
vellum-wrapped
invitations, page 62.

wording formal and semiformal invitations

- There is no punctuation other than a comma after the day of the week and city and periods after abbreviations, such as Mr. and Mrs.

- Capitalize only proper nouns, such as titles, names, day of the week, month, and location names.

- All dates and times are spelled out rather than using numbers. Times are followed by "o'clock." The abbreviations a.m. and p.m. are not used. If there might be confusion as to the time of day, you can add "in the evening" after the time.

- The address of the place of worship is not included unless it is in a big city and may be unfamiliar to the guests. Such information could be included on an insert.

- Do not mention gifts in the invitation. Gift registry information should be given by word of mouth to those who inquire.

- Use the appropriate titles before names, such as Mr., Mrs., Miss, Ms., Lieutenant, Reverend, Fr., etc. Spell out Doctor unless the name that follows is very long.

Mr. and Mrs. Greggory Dale
request the honour of your presence
at the marriage of their daughter
Jennifer Lee
to
Mr. Robert David Jensen
Saturday, the twenty-eighth of June
two thousand and three
at four o'clock
United Methodist Church
New Ulm, Minnesota

FORMAL WEDDING
HOSTED BY THE BRIDE'S
MARRIED PARENTS

Mr. Greggory Dale and Mrs. Liza Jeffers
request the honour of your presence
at the marriage of their daughter
Jennifer Lee
to
Mr. Robert David Jensen
Saturday, the twenty-eighth of June
two thousand and three
at four o'clock
United Methodist Church
New Ulm, Minnesota

FORMAL WEDDING
HOSTED BY THE BRIDE'S
DIVORCED PARENTS

Mr. and Mrs. Greggory Dale
and
Mr. and Mrs. William Jensen
request the honour of your presence
at the marriage of their children
Jennifer Lee Dale
and
Mr. Robert David Jensen
Saturday, the twenty-eighth of June
two thousand and three
at four o'clock
United Methodist Church
New Ulm, Minnesota

FORMAL WEDDING
HOSTED BY THE BRIDE'S AND
GROOM'S PARENTS

Miss Jennifer Lee Dale
and
Mr. Robert David Jensen
request the honour of your presence
at their marriage
Saturday, the twenty-eighth of June
two thousand and three
at four o'clock
United Methodist Church
New Ulm, Minnesota

FORMAL WEDDING
HOSTED BY THE BRIDE
AND GROOM

enclosures and addressing

POSSIBLE ENCLOSURES

- Response cards with stamped return envelopes

- At-home cards giving your guests your new address

- Maps to the ceremony and reception

- Pew cards for assigned seating at the ceremony

- Reception invitations if the ceremony and reception are held in different places

- Tissues, once used to prevent ink from smearing, are now merely decorative

OUTER ENVELOPES

- Address both members of a married couple, for example as Mr. and Mrs. Luke Walker if the wife has taken the husband's last name or as Mr. Luke Walker and Ms. Grace Nesbit if the wife kept her maiden name. If widowed, Mrs. Luke Walker; if divorced, Mrs. Grace Walker.

- If the invitation is to an unmarried couple, list their names on separate lines in alphabetical order.

- If you are inviting a single guest to bring a date, the outer envelope is addressed only to the invited guest; the inner envelope would say James Fischer and Guest.

- When including children of the invited couple, write out their names on a line under the parents, rather than use "and family." If over 13, use the proper title, such as Miss Alison Walker. If under 13, simply Alison. Children over 18 should receive their own invitation.

- Send invitations to all the attendants and ceremony participants, even though they are fully aware of your wedding.

- Use no abbreviations other than titles, such as Mr. and Mrs.

INNER ENVELOPES

- List only the guest's names on the inner envelopes; no addresses.

- Use family names for close relatives, if you wish, such as Uncle Jack and Aunt Denise.

INVITATION BASICS

Begin shopping for your invitations at least six months before the wedding. Even if you want to make your own invitations, make a sample this early in the planning to be sure you will be happy with the results. Printers usually need at least four weeks to process orders, and you should allow yourself a month to address them. If possible, get the inner and outer envelopes ahead of time so that you can begin addressing them right away. It is a good idea to have the outer envelope flaps printed with your return address in case guests' addresses have changed. Mail the invitations about six weeks before the wedding.

Address the envelopes before inserting the invitation and enclosures to prevent imprinting on them. At left are are a few etiquette guidelines to follow when addressing the invitations.

To assemble your invitations, arrange each of the elements in a separate stack in the order they will be picked up. If your invitation has a single fold with the message on the inside, place the enclosures inside the invitation. For single layer or single-fold invitations with the message on the front, the enclosures are placed in front of the invitation. The invitation and enclosures are then placed into the inner envelope. Single-fold invitations are inserted with the fold down and the front facing away from you. Single layer invitations are inserted with the message facing you. The inner envelope is left unsealed and placed into the outer envelope bottom first with the names facing you. Before sealing the outer envelope, make sure the names on the envelopes match! Take a completed invitation to the post office and have it weighed for the necessary postage. Then buy pretty stamps that will complement your wedding style.

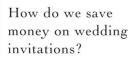

How do we save money on wedding invitations?

Avoid oversized or square invitations that require more postage.

Opt for thermography, rather than engraving. It is very similar but less expensive.

Limit enclosures. On less formal invitations, the reception information can be added after the ceremony information.

Don't use an inner envelope for semiformal and informal invitations.

Order about 25 extras in case of mistakes or oversights. Reprinting is costly.

Create the invitations at home on your computer. Or at least create the enclosures.

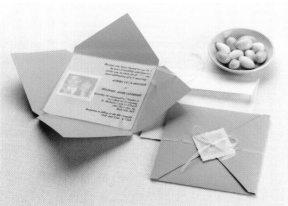

If your heart is set on square invitations, save some money by creating them at home on your computer, page 63.

legal matters

WHATEVER YOU DO, REMEMBER THE LICENSE! Research the requirements for your area and take care of any other legal matters well ahead of time.

MARRIAGE LICENSE

A marriage license is actually a permit confirming that the bride and groom are free to marry each other—that they are of legal age, that neither is legally bound to another in marriage, and both have obtained any necessary blood tests. The requirements for obtaining a marriage license and the pick-up location vary from state to state. Start your research by looking in the phone book under county government in the county where the ceremony will be held.

If you are planning a foreign destination wedding, you will need to research the requirements for that location and make sure that the marriage will be legally binding at home.

NAME AND MARITAL STATUS CHANGES

The bride has three options concerning her last name—she can take her husband's last name, retain her own, or hyphenate her own and her husband's last names. Whichever option she chooses becomes legally binding when she signs it on her marriage license. When a name change occurs, several people, agencies, and organizations must be notified. They include the Social Security Administration, state motor vehicles department, passport agency, employer payroll departments, banks and credit unions, mortgage companies, credit card companies, and voter registration. You may also add to that list any religious and academic affiliations, your doctors, and your dentists.

Before your marriage, you should also discuss how your finances will be handled. Will you have separate or joint savings and checking accounts? Will you share equally in bill-paying responsibilities? It is wise to put your wills and finances in order. Make any necessary changes on your existing insurance policies and retirement plans, including beneficiaries. Also contact your employers to adjust the federal and state deductions being taken from your paychecks.

marriage license questions

- What is the valid window of time?
- Is there a waiting period?
- What are the residency requirements?
- Do you need an appointment to apply?
- What documents are required?
- Do bride and groom both need to be present to apply?
- What is the fee?

hiring service professionals

DURING YOUR PLANNING YOU WILL INTERVIEW AND HIRE VARIOUS WEDDING professionals. Knowing what questions to ask and the proper way to handle contracts and payments will make the job easier and avoid disappointments.

ASK THE RIGHT QUESTIONS

Interview forms for interviewing vendors, such as florists, bakers, caterers, and photographers begin on page 116. Make copies of the forms for every person or group you are considering. These forms will help you compare services and prices and make informed decisions. It is important to get at least three references from each vendor and to follow up with phone calls.

GET IT IN WRITING

Get a letter of agreement or contract with each service provider you choose. If they do not initiate one, write one yourself and ask them to sign it. You can use the planning forms in this book as a basis for writing the contracts. Be sure to include all the details. If you have not made final decisions about details, such as exactly what flowers you want in your bouquet, you can set a maximum or general amount in the initial contract with the statement that details will be confirmed in writing by a certain date. Before signing a contract written up by a vendor, read it thoroughly. If you don't agree with any part of it, ask to change it. If your request is reasonable and the vendor will not comply, look elsewhere. Know exactly what you are paying for, whether or not gratuities have been included, how and when payments are to be made. Look for hidden charges, such as overtime fees or packages that include services you do not need or want. Document every wedding arrangement you make. Include the day, date, and time of your wedding with the exact location of the site and details about delivery and setup times.

> Know exactly what you are paying for, whether or not gratuities have been included, how and when payments are to be made.

PAYING

Pay deposits with a credit card and make the smallest deposits possible so you will be better able to dispute any charges for services that were unsatisfactory or withhold payments for damaged goods. Check with your credit card company for such options. Always get a receipt for every payment made and keep your receipts together in the folders at the back of this planner. Keep accurate records of bills owed, payments made, and final payments due.

REFUNDS

Written into every contract should be a refund policy that states exactly what refund you will receive if you cancel and what penalty the service provider will pay if they cancel.

ceremony details

YOUR WEDDING CEREMONY IS A PROFOUNDLY significant event in your life. It should be a personal statement of your commitment to each other. Though the basic structure of most ceremonies is similar, you can choose the music, readings, added rituals, and personal vows to make yours unique. With your wedding gown and the choices you make for your attendants' attire, together with the flowers and other decorations, you can bring to reality the image you've created in your mind of the perfect wedding day. And just in case you happen to blink, a photographer and videographer can capture every moment for you to relive over and over!

bridal attire

YOUR WEDDING GOWN SHOULD BE THE DRESS OF YOUR DREAMS. WHILE flattering you in every way, it should reflect your personal style, move gracefully with you up and down the aisle and around the dance floor, and fit to perfection.

SHOPPING FOR YOUR GOWN

Making the right choice may seem like a daunting task, especially when you gaze upon that sea of white the first time you enter a bridal salon. But, the perfect dress for you is out there and you will find it. Give yourself a head start by looking through bridal fashion magazines and tearing out pictures of the gowns that catch your eye. You may find that you are

attracted to a certain dress shape, neckline, or waist feature. Maybe intricate details are important to you, or maybe you prefer a sleek, minimalist look. Study your favorite photos and jot down what you really like about each one. Then take your pictures with you and start shopping. Also take a copy of the wedding attire shopping worksheet on page 128 if you are considering several options.

In most cities there are several kinds of stores that carry bridal gowns. Full-service bridal shops carry moderate to high end dresses and a full range of accessories for the bride and her attendants. A sales assistant can direct you to the styles that would be most flattering for you. While it may be possible to buy a dress off the rack, usually the store will order a new dress for you and have it custom-fit in their own alterations department. You can expect a lot of personal attention and the convenience of doing all your shopping in one place.

If you are able to spend the money for a custom designed gown, consider a couture shop or an independent custom gown designer. A couture shop can offer you high-end, exclusive designer dresses, cut and sewn specifically to your own measurements. An independent designer can blend your desires with his or her ideas and design flair and create a one-of-a-kind gown.

Gowns can also be purchased from some higher-end department stores, where

SHEATH

EMPIRE

dress types

A sheath dress has a slim silhouette, closely following the lines of the body. It is flattering to slim brides who are either tall or petite. This silhouette should be avoided by full-figured or pear-shaped brides.

An empire gown has a high "waistline" just under the bust. From there the skirt opens gradually into a moderate A-line or fuller shape. This silhouette elongates your figure, making it a good choice for a petite bride or someone with a short or thick waist. If you are a classic hour-glass figure, an empire waist could hide some of your best features.

An A-line or princess design has vertical seams that run from the shoulders, over the bust, and down into a flared skirt, creating an A-shaped silhouette. This is a flattering silhouette for an hourglass figure or someone with a short waist, but should be avoided if you have a thick or undefined waist.

The ball gown silhouette has a full-length, fitted bodice and a very full skirt. The most popular silhouette, a ball gown is perfect for tall, slender brides as well as full-figured types, but may overwhelm a petite bride.

PRINCESS

BALL GOWN

you can browse on your own or request personalized service. If a store doesn't have a dress in your size, they can usually have one transferred from another store. You can then opt to have alterations done in the store or buy the dress and find a seamstress.

If you are under a time crunch or want to save money and sacrifice personal service, shop discount bridal outlets and national bridal chain stores. Discount outlets usually carry discontinued national brands and private label gowns at reduced prices. Chain stores usually carry their own private label gowns, which means lower prices and a more limited selection. You will probably browse without much sales assistance, buy off the rack, and take care of your own alterations. This could mean that your new dress needs

cleaning before you wear it—a hidden cost. But you may still find the dress of your dreams.

Not every bride wants to spend a small fortune on a dress that is worn once. You also have the option of renting a wedding dress from a clothing rental store. The selection will be limited and a perfect fit could be a problem, but a good rental shop should be able to provide you with a like-new gown.

FLATTERING SILHOUETTES

Wedding dresses are designed in four basic silhouettes (shown above) with elements that highlight positive figure features and hide imperfections. By analyzing your figure, you can decide which silhouette will be most flattering for you.

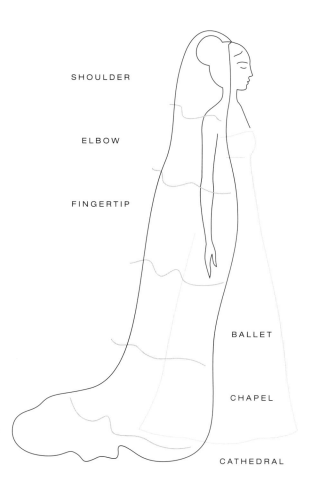

SHOULDER

ELBOW

FINGERTIP

BALLET

CHAPEL

CATHEDRAL

veil types

- Shoulder or flyaway veils touch the shoulders. This is the usual length for a blusher veil, worn over the face during the processional.

- Elbow length veils touch the elbows when the arms are straight at the sides.

- Fingertip veils touch the fingertips when the arms are straight at the sides.

- Ballet or waltz length veils fall to mid-calf or just above the ankles.

- Chapel length veils brush the floor.

- Cathedral length veils trail on the floor three to five yards from the headpiece.

DEGREES OF FORMALITY

In choosing a gown, also consider the formality of your wedding. If you are having a formal evening wedding in a house of worship, you should look for a gown that has a train. The longer the train, the more formal the gown. The formal gown will probably be made of a formal fabric such as satin, lace, or silk shantung. A less formal daytime wedding calls for a less formal style, such as a floor-length or tea-length dress in chiffon, organza, or taffeta. Some fabrics are more appropriate for different seasons, such as velvet in winter or linen in summer.

ALTERATION SAVVY

Your gown will probably require alterations in order to fit you perfectly. You can schedule appointments for fittings when you order the gown, giving you enough time to have alterations completed in time but not so early that you might gain or lose enough weight to make a difference in the fit. Take along the shoes and undergarments you will be wearing for every appointment as they make a big difference in how the dress fits. If you are unsure about which foundation garments will work best, the first fitting appointment is the time to try them on and make that decision.

THE PERFECT HEADPIECE AND VEIL

The first rule for choosing or designing head attire is that it must complement your dress; be consistent with the dress's style (traditional, contemporary, or period) and formality. Some designers manufacture head attire to coordinate with their gowns, but that doesn't mean their veils are necessarily perfect for the bride who buys the dress. The real purpose of your headpiece and veil is to bring the focal point of the ensemble to your face, flattering you in every way.

The headpiece should enhance your bone structure and facial proportions, highlight your best features and camouflage your flaws. Just like different hair styles, some headpieces add height or elongate your face; others make your face appear wider. Details at the temples draw attention to your eyes. Begin by deciding how you will wear your

hair for the wedding. Then, wearing your hair in the same general style, try on various headpieces to decide what shape is right for you.

There are many veil styles to choose from. They vary in length, fullness, in the shape in which they are cut, in the attachment point to the headpiece, and in embellishment. Consider the silhouette you want the veil to create, in combination with the dress. Veils falls into several standard categories by length; the length you select is influenced by the style of the gown and the formality of the wedding. Full-skirted gowns are better balanced with longer veils; sleek dress silhouettes look better with shorter veils. In general, longer veils are worn for more formal weddings, in grand or solemn settings with a feeling of pageantry. Shorter veils are more casual and unconventional; they are also suitable for second-time brides.

Veils can be a single tier, double tier, or triple tier. Two- and three-tier veils can be made so all the tiers fall to the same length, or each tier can fall to one of the standard lengths; the longest tier being the bottom layer and the shortest being the top layer.

For a perfect headpiece and veil at a fraction of the store-bought price, consider making your own. All the supplies you need are available at the bridal department of fabric stores. There are even styles that require no machine sewing. Make the headpiece and veil on page 68 or design your own.

ACCESSORIES

You may choose to accessorize your bridal ensemble with a simple pearl or diamond necklace and matching earrings. Bracelets, watches and rings other than your engagement ring (worn on the right hand until after the ceremony) are usually not worn on your wedding day. Gloves can really dress up your ensemble. They come in various lengths, which you choose depending on whether or not your gown has sleeves and the style and length of the sleeves. Short gloves can simply be removed for the ring exchange. When long gloves are worn, the ring finger can be slipped out of an opening made in the glove finger seam. Some gloves are fingerless, making the ring exchange easier. Select shoes that complement the gown style, with extra attention to comfort. Take time before the wedding to break them in and scuff the soles if they tend to slip around.

Take care in selecting your hose, especially if there will be dancing. Buy an extra pair to keep in your emergency kit. If you are getting married in a cool or cold weather season, you may want to buy a shawl or stole or look into renting a floor-length white fur wrap. Your accessories are one way to include the "something old, borrowed, and blue" elements of your outfit, assuming the "new" is your gown.

Save money by creating your own headpiece and veil (above, left), page 68. Accessories like a penny pocket (above) and keepsake garter (left), pages 70 and 71, make your wedding attire special.

dressing the attendants

HOW WILL YOU DRESS YOUR ROW OF PRETTY MAIDS? THIS TASK COULD prove to be more difficult than choosing your own attire, unless your attendants are your identical quadruplet sisters.

PLEASING EVERYONE

You selected your attendants because they are your dear friends or relatives. It is very possible that in the group there are various body types and sizes, skin tones, and hair colors, which means that no one particular dress silhouette and color will be perfect for all of them. Add to these considerations the expenses your attendants will incur. You want their dresses to be affordable because they also have to pay for shoes and accessories to round out the ensembles, parties, shower gifts, and a wedding gift for you. The situation takes strategy and tact, but in the end, they will all look great in your wedding photos!

Your bridesmaids' dresses should match yours in their degree of formality, and the fabrics should complement each other. You can approach the task of selecting dresses in a number of ways. You can choose to dress the bridesmaids in identical dresses of your favorite color because that is what you have had your heart set on forever. You might choose a silhouette that flatters most figure types, such as an A-line or empire style, or select a two-piece dress so that tops and skirts can be fitted separately. A trend is to dress them all in the same fabric in a universally "friendly" color, but in different dress styles to best suit their unique qualities. Another approach is to select the same dress design for all of them, but dress them in a family of colors that flatter each individually.

Each of your attendants should go to the store to be measured so the store can order dresses for them in the sizes that will require the least alteration.

COORDINATING EFFORTS

If you value your maid of honor's opinion and sense of style, ask her to help you with your initial search. Each of your attendants should go to the store to be measured so the store can order dresses for them in the sizes that will require the least alteration. For some fabrics, this may mean a larger size should be ordered and taken in rather than risk unsightly needle holes and unremovable crease lines where seams must be let out. The store can then order all the dresses at once, assuring the same dye lot if the dresses are all the same color.

If possible, have all the alterations made by the same person, so that fit and hem length will be uniform. Otherwise make sure that you have communicated your desires to each of them so they are all working toward the same goal. For floor-length dresses, hemlines should all be measured the same distance from the floor when the bridesmaids are wearing their wedding day shoes. If any of your maids are particularly tall, make sure (in writing) when the dresses are ordered that extra length is allowed in their skirts. Otherwise their dresses may arrive already too short, making it necessary for all the other dresses to be hemmed too short also. For less casual lengths, hems should fall to the same location on their legs; tea-length on a tall woman is not the same distance from the floor as it is for a petite woman.

Shoes should be selected for their comfort and style. If you have chosen to dress your bridesmaids identically, they should all probably wear the same shoe style (closed or open toe, strappy or not), perhaps in different heel heights if necessary. If you want to have them dyed to match, the shoes should be taken in for dyeing together, with a swatch of the dress fabric for matching. If they will be wearing different dress styles or colors, you might designate certain style features for uniformity and allow them to select their own shoes. They should all wear their wedding-day shoes to their fitting appointments.

CHILD ATTENDANTS

Junior bridesmaids are usually dressed in the same fabric and color as the older bridesmaids. They can wear the same style of dress or a similar style more appropriate for their age. The flower girl may be dressed to look like a mini-bride, wearing a white ballet-length dress with a full skirt. Otherwise, she wears a dress of the same fabric and color as the bridesmaids, but in a style suitable for a child. The parents of the child attendants pay for their daughters' dresses.

HAIRSTYLES AND ACCESSORIES

Your bridesmaids' usual hairstyles are probably as diverse as their personalities, so it may be awkward or impossible to ask them to wear their hair in the same style. And why would you want them to, when the trend is toward stressing their individuality? You might ask that long hair be worn in an updo in keeping with the formality of the occasion, which may require salon appointments. Women with shorter hair may be proficient at styling their own hair, and salon appointments would only add to their expenses. Use careful consideration and tact to determine a hairstyle plan. If you want them to wear something on their heads, such as a headpiece, floral barrette, or beaded hair picks, or if a headpiece is required by your religion, also consider the placement and attachment method for each of them.

Other accessories you choose for your attendants can make them look like a more unified group, especially if they are wearing different dress styles or colors. As your gifts to them, you might present your attendants with matching necklaces and earrings to be worn on the wedding day. Other accessories, like gloves or shawls are purchased by the bridesmaids. Gloves and head attire add to the formality of the total ensemble. If you are considering shawls, keep in mind that they should fall to uniform lengths and that it may take some practice to get used to wearing them without constant adjustment.

Make a keepsake for your flower girl, page 77.

dressing the men

THE MEN IN THE WEDDING PARTY HAVE EASIER DECISIONS TO MAKE AND far fewer options from which to choose. If only all of your wedding plans were this simple!

STYLE FOR THE BIG GUYS

The groom and his attendants, and often the bride's and groom's fathers, dress to suit the occasion. Unless the wedding is quite casual, they usually rent their attire from a formal-wear shop. So, once you have selected their outfit for them, all they need to do is get fitted, pick it up, and return it. Your selection depends on the time, location, and degree of formality of the wedding. General selection guidelines are provided opposite.

STYLE FOR THE LITTLE GUYS

The ring bearer, train bearers, or pages can be dressed like the older men or in a style more appropriate for a child. Depending on the season, you may choose to dress a small boy in shorts and a jacket or in a suit. If he wears a white suit or shorts, he should also wear white socks and shoes. If he wears a dark suit, he should wear dark socks and black shoes.

Make a ring bearer pillow (below), page 78, or a best man's ring pouch (opposite), page 80, from your grandmother's handkerchief.

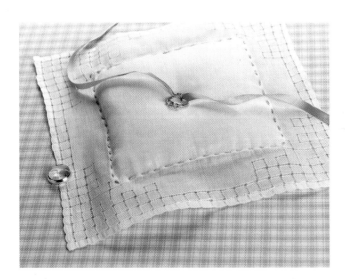

RENTAL ARRANGEMENTS

Make your selections, including accessories and shoes, about three or four months before the wedding and reserve the formalwear in the sizes needed. Early reservations are especially important if the wedding is in April or May—prom season. Each of the men will need to go in a for a fitting or have someone take accurate measurements and send them to the store. Each man is responsible for picking up, paying for, and returning his own formalwear. If you will be leaving for your honeymoon immediately after the wedding, make sure someone is designated to return the groom's outfit. If any of the groomsmen will be coming in from out of town, you also may need to make other arrangements for them.

how do you wear this thing?

Cummerbunds are worn with the pleats opening upward. Worn over the trouser waistband, a functional cummerbund does more than hold in a paunch. It has a small pocket built into one of the pleats on the right side where one can stow a tip for the maître d' or a couple of breath mints.

general criteria for menswear

- For an ultraformal evening wedding, the groom and his attendants should wear black tailcoats, black trousers, stiff white wing-collar shirts with studs and cufflinks, black cummerbunds or vests, and a white bow tie.

- An ultraformal daytime wedding calls for black or gray cutaway coats, black or gray striped trousers, stiff white shirts with fold-down collars, gray vests, and ascots. For extra style, you can add a top hat, spats, and gray gloves.

- For a formal evening wedding, classic black tuxedos are in order. They are worn with a white wing or spread-collar shirt, black bow tie or four-in-hand tie, and matching vest or cummerbund. During the summer or in a warm climate, the men could wear white dinner jackets with formal trousers.

- There are several choices for a formal daytime wedding, including classic tuxedos, tailcots, and gray strollers. They can be worn with a white spread-collar shirt, a vest to match the jacket, and an ascot or four-in-hand tie.

- For a semiformal or casual evening wedding, the men can wear either dark tuxedos with vests or cummerbunds or matching dark suits. White shirts with turned-down collars are worn with bow ties or neckties. In warm weather, white dinner jackets are another option.

- For a semiformal or casual daytime wedding, men can wear suits with white shirts and neckties. Navy or dark gray are suitable anytime; khaki works well in summer. Depending on how casual you want to be, you may even omit the tie.

ceremony structure

THOUGH THE ACTUAL CEREMONY MAY LAST LESS THAN AN HOUR, IT IS the main event of your wedding. Months of planning and preparation culminate in these few minutes.

Marriage is the legal union of a man and a woman as husband and wife. Whether your wedding is a civil service in a Las Vegas "wedding chapel," a formal religious service in a cathedral, or a cultural celebration in your own back yard, if you meet the legal requirements for marriage and the ceremony is conducted by a licensed officiant, you are married.

SEATING AND PROCESSIONAL

There are traditional methods for seating the guests and preparing for the ceremony. As guests arrive, the ushers greet them, hand them a wedding program, and then lead them to their seats. Traditionally, in Christian weddings the bride's friends and family are seated on the left and the groom's on the right. In Jewish weddings, the sides are reversed. Often, the guests are simply seated on either side, filling the rows evenly from the third or fourth row in front to the back. During this time, the organist, pianist, or

All eyes are on the bride as she enters, escorted by her father or another close male relative or friend.

other musician could be playing prelude music. If there are candles, they can be lit anytime before the honored guests are seated. Honor seating in the first three rows on each side is reserved for family members and other special guests, who are seated in this order: special guests, the groom's grandparents, the bride's grandparents, the groom's parents, and the bride's mother. The mothers of the bride and groom may be escorted by specially appointed ushers, such as their sons, or by the groom himself. After the bride's mother is seated, aisle ribbons may be drawn up the center aisle, closing off the rows and an aisle runner can be unrolled up to the foot of the altar in preparation for the processional.

Create your own wedding program, page 66.

Wedding participants enter in a slow-paced march called the processional, which is usually accompanied by special music. The officiant may be the first to enter, either down the aisle or from chambers off to the side of the altar. The groom and his best man enter and take their places at the head of the aisle on the right side, facing the guests, with the best man to the groom's left. The remaining ushers and groomsmen lead the procession, walking in pairs to the front and taking their place to the left of the best man. The bridesmaids enter, in pairs or singly, followed by the maid of honor and then the ring bearer and flower girl. At this point, the music changes to the bride's processional and the mother of the bride rises, signalling the guests to do the same. All eyes are on the bride as she enters, escorted by her father or another close male relative or friend. The ceremony begins and follows the general order at right.

RECESSIONAL

As the recessional music begins, the bride and groom walk back up the aisle, followed by their attendants in pairs. The maid of honor is escorted by the best man; the other bridesmaids by groomsmen. By this time the flower girl and ring bearer are usually sitting with their parents, and will exit with them later. The ushers return to the front and escort the honored guests from their seats. If aisle ribbons were used, they are then removed and the other guests are ushered out while the musician plays postlude music. Sometimes the bride and groom return and usher their guests out, giving everyone a chance to congratulate them and omitting the need for a receiving line later.

the ceremony

INTRODUCTION, INVOCATION, OR OPENING The officiant addresses the guests and announces the purpose of the gathering, to join the bride and groom (by name) in marriage. The guests are invited to participate by their presence, their thoughts, and perhaps their prayers.

MAIN BODY The officiant talks about the meaning of marriage and about the importance of your particular decision to wed. Often the main body is divided into the interrogation and the presentation. In the interrogation, the officiant asks the bride and groom if they have come of their own free will to be wed. This is also the part where the officiant says, "If anyone has just cause why these two may not wed, speak now or forever hold your peace." During the presentation, the bride is presented for marriage by her parents after the officiant asks, "Who gives this woman to be married?"

INTRODUCTION TO THE VOWS The officiant explains the importance of the vows which the bride and groom are about to exchange.

VOWS The bride and groom individually express their commitment by reading vows they have written or by responding "I do" or "I will" to questions posed by the officiant.

EXCHANGE OF RINGS The bride and groom take turns repeating phrases of commitment at the officiant's direction while placing a wedding ring on the left hand of their betrothed.

CLOSING AND ANNOUNCEMENT OF THE COUPLE The officiant announces that the bride and groom are officially married. This section may include a final prayer or benediction. The newlyweds are introduced for the first time as husband and wife and are invited to share their first married kiss.

Make your ceremony
unique. Include a symbolic
element like the lighting
of a unity candle, page 81.

MAKING YOUR CEREMONY PERSONAL

The traditional, religious, cultural, and personal elements that you include in your wedding ceremony make it your own. You may want to include symbolic elements, such as the lighting of the unity candle, presenting roses to your mothers, or breaking a glass. During the main body of the ceremony, you might include a speech, sermon or homily, and religious or secular readings by people of your choice. Consider prose and poetry as well as scriptural passages, and have them read by close friends or relatives. Musical selections, both instrumental and vocal, are always a meaningful addition to the ceremony. You may want to write your own vows, rather than follow the scripted ones. If yours will be a religious ceremony, consult with the officiant about what may or may not be allowed by your particular religion, in your particular site. Ask your officiant to indicate places in the ceremony where you can include these other elements.

ceremony music

MUSIC HAS THE POWER TO STIR UP EMOTIONS and add drama. While your decorations, flowers, and wedding attire make your wedding look beautiful, it is the music that makes it feel beautiful.

Consider how a movie's musical score can engage an audience and make them feel excitement, sorrow, happiness, or fear at any given moment. In much the same way, you can use music to set the tone and convey various feelings throughout your ceremony. At different times, you may want to convey anticipation, romance, grandeur, reverence, or joy. The musical selections and how they are used for different parts of the ceremony can make your guests feel welcome, involve them in the spirit of the occasion, and create lasting memories of your wedding.

Before you start making a list of your favorite tunes, ask your officiant if there are any restrictions or guidelines to be followed. Find out if you must adhere strictly to sacred music or if classical and modern music are appropriate and welcome as well. Some houses of worship may also require that you use their organist and vocalists rather than your own. Your officiant may have suggestions, and there are several traditional selections that you could use. There are many wedding music web sites on the Internet that list the titles and composers and even let you listen to the music. Be true to yourselves, and select music that you like.

While you are making your selections, also decide how and by whom they will be performed. Different instruments have different emotional effects. Strings are elegant and romantic, a brass band can be celebratory and jubilant, flute music feels joyful and lighthearted, organ music feels reverent and more formal than piano music. You can ask talented friends and relatives to play or sing during your wedding, or you have the option of hiring musicians and vocalists, if your budget will allow. Depending on the site and the formality of the wedding, you might even consider taped music.

times for music

THE PRELUDE Beginning about a half hour before the ceremony while the guests are being seated, various selections can be performed. Think of this time as a sneak preview of the event and as a time to welcome your guests and set the wedding tone.

THE PROCESSIONAL Right after the mother of the bride is seated, the music switches to something joyful and uplifting as the attendants begin to process down the aisle. Consider the time it will take for all of them to enter and take their places in front of the guests, and select music that fills that time span or can be repeated as many times as necessary.

THE BRIDE'S PROCESSIONAL As the bride's mother stands, the music switches to a dramatic selection that will accompany the bride as she walks down the aisle. Probably the most majestic music of the ceremony, it sets the stage for the momentous event that is about to begin.

DURING THE CEREMONY Your officiant can indicate to you a few times during the ceremony when instrumental and vocal selections would fit in nicely. You can decide how many and what kind of music you would like to hear. These selections should reflect the mood you are feeling and want to convey to your guests. At one point that might include a reverent, prayerful selection and at another a lighthearted, romantic song.

THE RECESSIONAL Think excitement! You have just been introduced as husband and wife, and it is very possible that your guests are standing in ovation. This music should be loud and jubilant as you walk arm in arm back up the aisle. The selection continues until all of your attendants have walked out also.

THE POSTLUDE This music is played while the guests are being ushered out or are moving through the receiving line. It can include various kinds of happy music, much like the selections played during the prelude.

Seasonal flowers can be cut closer to the time they are used, so they will stay fresher longer and be more fragrant.

flowers

WOULD IT BE A WEDDING WITHOUT FLOWERS? FRAGRANT, COLORFUL blossoms punctuate the ceremony and reception with festivity. By their color and arrangement, they give your wedding particular style.

WHAT'S YOUR STYLE?

The flowers you select for your wedding help establish the theme, whether it be formal or casual, traditional or contemporary, nostalgic or avant-garde. Before you shop for a florist, spend some time looking through bridal and home interior magazines, surfing floral websites, and looking through gardening books to get some ideas about the kinds of flowers you would like for your wedding. A florist experienced in wedding design can help you choose flowers that express the degree of formality you want, work well in the ceremony and reception sites you have selected, and complement the wedding attire. Use the florist interview form on page 120 when you shop for a florist to help you ask the right questions and decide which florist is right for your wedding.

SEASONAL PICKS

There are advantages to choosing flowers that are in season or readily available year-round. Though many flowers can now be shipped from other countries or forced in green-houses all year, it is more affordable to use flowers that are naturally in season. Also, seasonal flowers can be cut closer to the time they are used, so they will stay fresher longer and be more fragrant. It is also more likely that certain seasonal flowers will fit the style of your wedding. For instance, lilacs seem out of place in winter and asters seem out of place in spring. Flower varieties that are readily available and consistently priced year-round include rose, orchid, lily, delphinium, carnation, alstromeria, calla lily, freesia, stephanotis, snapdragon, and baby's breath. Springtime flowers are apple and cherry blossoms, forsythia, iris, lilac, lily of the valley, tulip, violet, hyacinth, heather, pussy willow, sweet pea, and peony varieties. In summer, good choices include dahlia, geranium, hydrangea, daisy, foxglove, gladiolus, poppy, sunflower, protea, Queen Anne's lace, calla lily, and larkspur. Autumn weddings are often decorated with aster, chrysanthemum, zinnia, bittersweet, dahlia, yarrow, and daisy varieties. In winter, consider evergreens, cyclamen, amaryllis, holly, pepperberry, Star of Bethlehem, and statice.

Christmas, Easter, Mother's Day, and Valentine's Day place great demands on the supply of many flower types, so if your wedding is near one of these days, you may have to select alternatives that can be substituted if necessary. Also, flower prices skyrocket at these times.

color choices

- Your florist can help you choose the color scheme you want to create with the flowers.

- A monochromatic scheme includes flowers of various sizes and textures in several shades of the same color.

- Analogous color schemes include flowers in colors that are adjacent to each other on the color wheel. For example, you might choose blossoms in shades of blue, blue-violet, and violet.

- For a complementary scheme, you might select two or three flowers in different shades of your favorite color and accent them with a few blossoms and sprigs in their complementary color, directly opposite them on the color wheel.

- Triadic color schemes include flowers in three colors equally spaced around the color wheel, such as red, yellow, and blue, perhaps with a little white included to spark up the colors.

- Flower colors are usually selected after you have ordered the bridesmaids' dresses, and both elements combine to create your wedding color scheme.

Make hair wreaths (below), page 76, boutonnieres and corsages (below), page 74, or bouquets (opposite), page 72, to save money.

MAKING YOUR WISH LIST

By the time you select a florist, you should know your floral budget, the number of attendants, and the estimated guest count. You should also have selected ceremony and reception sites and have consulted with the managers of the sites to see if there are any restrictions or provisions concerning flowers. Some religious venues, for example, do not allow you to bring in floral decorations or have restrictions on where arrangements can be placed. Others may have available portable candelabras or urns that you may decorate with flowers. There may be large stationary potted plants that will be part of the décor. A visit to the sites will help you visualize where floral arrangements would be most effective, how many you should have, and how large they should be.

With this information gathered, you are ready to make your list. Begin with the items you must include, such as the bride's bouquet; a tossing bouquet; boutonnieres for the groom and his attendants, fathers, grandfathers, and any other male ceremony participants; and bouquets or single flowers for the bridesmaids. If you have a flower girl, she will need something floral to carry and perhaps flowers in her hair. Mothers, grandmothers, readers, and other female participants should have a corsage. Next list all of the floral arrangements you might want in the ceremony and reception sites. Include flowers at the entrances, to dress up the pews or chair rows, to adorn the altar, and for the buffet tables, head table, and the guest tables. Then add the items you would like to include if you can afford them, such as a floral arbor to walk through, a floral accent on the cake knife, a floral cake topper, rose petals for your guests to shower you with as you leave the

how can we save money on flowers?

Your florist can suggest lower cost alternatives for all your floral needs.

Centerpieces and bouquets can be plumped up with less expensive accent flowers and greenery.

Delegate someone to transport flowers from the ceremony site to be used again at the reception.

Use the bride's and bridesmaids' bouquets to decorate the head table when you arrive at the reception.

Depending on the season and theme, you could create centerpieces of fresh fruit, vegetables, or inexpensive potted plants.

Use candlelight and mirrors to amplify the effect of fewer or smaller floral arrangements.

If you or someone close to you is an avid gardener, you could create some or all of your own arrangements and centerpieces.

Rent large potted plants from a nursery.

ceremony. Use the planning guide on page 120 to help you make your list. After consulting with the florist, fill in prices for each of the items, and then review the list and see how far your budget will stretch.

There are several ways to make your floral budget go farther, such as doing some of the work yourself. You can, for instance, make boutonnieres and corsages yourself or with the help of a friend. Directions are on pages 74 and 75. You could choose to make hand-tied bouquets for yourself and your bridesmaids, following the directions on page 72. Your flower girl could carry a basket of fresh flowers that you have arranged (page 77) and wear a hand-made floral wreath in her hair (page 76). Silk flowers can be substituted for fresh flowers and used for arrangements you can make yourself or with your bridesmaids weeks before the wedding. They might include a door bouquet (page 82), pew wreaths (page 83), wreaths to adorn the backs of the bride's and groom's chairs (page 86), and even floral centerpieces (page 88).

photography

YOU HAVE ONLY ONE CHANCE TO CAPTURE YOUR WEDDING ON FILM. YOU need a photographer who can preserve your wedding in pictures that reflect your style and personalities. Next to choosing your mate, choosing a photographer could be your most important decision.

PHOTOGRAPHIC STYLE

Photographers generally fit into one of three categories: traditional photographers, photojournalists, and those who can skillfully work in either style. Traditional photographers create portraits and posed shots that are well-lit and technically polished. They are accustomed to working in a studio where they can control the lighting. Photojournalists look for opportunities to "capture the moment" in candid shots that tell the wedding-day story. They often shoot in black-and-white as well as color. The best way to decide which photographic style you like is to look through albums of wedding photos taken in both styles.

FINDING THE RIGHT PHOTOGRAPHER

Family or friends who have recently married may be able to recommend photographers. Other wedding professionals, such as your caterer or florist, can suggest photographers with whom they have worked. If you have the opportunity to attend a bridal show in your area, you can meet photographers and look at their work. Any professional photographer who has ample wedding experience and great organizational skills should have a portfolio of work to show potential clients. While browsing through examples of the photographer's work, look for clear images, thoughtful compositions, and good lighting effects. Ideally, he or she will also be able to show you a complete wedding album. As you turn the pages, you should get a sense of the bride's and groom's personalities and the style of their wedding. The candid shots should convey emotions and catch people in natural, spontaneous positions. People in posed shots and portraits should look relaxed. In talking with the photographer, you should get a sense that every album he or she creates is uniquely suited to that particular couple and their wedding style.

Even the most skillful photographer isn't right for you if you don't feel totally comfortable with him or her. This is a person who will be in close contact with you and all of your guests. To get the best shots, a good photographer needs an assertive, friendly personality. He or she needs to be able to "work the crowd" and coax your guests into natural, easy smiles without seeming invasive. You will invite the photographer behind the scenes and into intimate moments between you and your attendants, family, and each other. You must feel relaxed and open with your photographer and not self-conscious about displaying your emotions in front of the camera. Your photographer should be eager to get to know you and learn about your wedding style and photo preferences.

The photographer interview form on page 122 will help you in the interviewing process. Be sure that the person you interview is the actual photographer who will work at your wedding. Confirm that this person is willing to follow your "must-take" list as well as find candid shots throughout the event. When you contact references, ask them if they would recommend this photographer to their best friends and ask why or why not. You will also want to know if the photographer was on time and well-dressed and had a good rapport with them and their guests. Find out if they were completely happy with their wedding album and if the final cost was as they had expected.

Even the most skillful photographer isn't right for you if you don't feel totally comfortable with him or her.

BEFORE YOU SIGN

Once you select your photographer, ask for an itemized list of costs. It should include his or her time spent at the wedding, an estimate of the number of shots to be taken, all post-production work, and assembling the album. Compare the estimate with your budget. If it is more than you had anticipated, ask the photographer where costs can be cut. Or look for ways to cut costs in other areas of your budget to free up more money for photography.

VIDEOGRAPHY

Wedding videos are gaining in popularity. They offer you the thrill of viewing your wedding like a movie, complete with sound and action. You can rewind your favorite romantic parts and giggle at the funny parts over and over. Wedding videography can range in price from $300 to $3,000, depending on the videographer's experience and degree of professionalism and the quality of the final product. Just like the photographer, your videographer has only one chance to get it right, so your selection process must be just as careful. An interview form for interviewing videographers is on page 123.

Before you begin looking, find out if there are any restrictions for videography at your ceremony site. Many churches and synagogues will not allow the videographer near the altar. If this is the case, you might decide that the cost is not worth it without capturing your faces as you say your vows and exchange your rings.

reception details

AFTER THE VOWS ARE SPOKEN AND IT'S TIME to celebrate, what kind of party do you want? The reception is a celebration of your love and marriage, but it is also your way of thanking your guests for their good will and generosity. Though the ceremony is the wedding focal point, organizing the reception will take far more of your time and money. Well-planned music can be both entertaining and mood-setting. A gorgeous wedding cake and a few decorations will help make your reception look beautiful. But most of your efforts and money will go for food and drink. Whether that means treating your guests to champagne and strawberries in a garden or hosting an open bar and a five-course seated meal at a country club, you want the event to be unique. With careful preparation and attention to the details, your wedding reception will complement the ceremony perfectly and make a memorable impression on you and your guests.

let the celebration begin!

YOUR FIRST SOCIAL UNDERTAKING AS HUSBAND AND WIFE IS TO HOST perhaps the biggest party of your life. Each and every guest craves a few moments of your time, while everyone revels in the joy that you share. Whether you have planned a sophisticated champagne brunch for fifty or a blowout, rock-and-roll-band bash for two hundred, the memories created in these few short hours will bring back smiles for years.

THE RICE SHOWER

The classic scene is the bride and groom dashing from the church to a waiting car through a shower of rice. This symbolic wish for fertility, prosperity, and good fortune has lasted through many changes, mainly concerning what is tossed. Over the years, rice has been criticized or forbidden for a number of reasons: people easily slip and fall on rice, it stings when it hits you in the face, it is harmful for birds, it is almost impossible to clean up, etc. Some opt for bird seed, but that can cause weeds to sprout unless you sterilize it first. For a few years, everyone seemed to be blowing bubbles as a safe, soft, clean alternative. Flower petals are always popular, though they could get costly for hundreds of guests. Now you have another option: designer wedding rice—processed rice that is shaped like little hearts and touted as safe for birds. There's still the matter of cleanup, however, and no matter what you decide your guests should toss, you must seek the approval of the site manager.

MAKING THE TRANSITION

Unless your ceremony and reception are held at the same location, you will need to arrange transportation for yourselves, your parents, and your attendants. If your budget permits and you want to go in high style, this could mean your own private horse and buggy and chauffeured limo rides for everyone else. The transportation interview form on page 127 will help you ask the right questions and make the arrangements. Grand scale isn't necessary or important to everyone, however. You may have friends and relatives who are willing to be a part of your celebration by helping out with the transportation. Just make sure arrangements are made ahead of time and everyone knows which cars they are riding in.

LAG TIME

Ideally you want your reception to begin within one hour after the ceremony. Often the formal wedding party photos are taken after the ceremony, partly because of the superstition that the groom's first sight of his bride in her gown should be when she walks toward him

down the aisle. So it is likely that your guests will begin arriving at the reception before you. It is a good idea to designate an honored couple, perhaps a close aunt and uncle, to serve as your reception hosts until your arrival, directing guests to the coat check and bar and encouraging them to mingle as they await your arrival. Even after you arrive, these "stand-in hosts" are a valuable asset to you and your parents, taking care of details and freeing you to enjoy the celebration. You should honor them with a corsage and boutonniere and be sure to thank them with a gift later.

RECEIVING LINE

Affording each of your guests the opportunity to congratulate you and wish you well is an important part of the celebration. Some couples choose to have their receiving line at the ceremony site, others upon their arrival at the reception. Couples who usher their own guests out of the ceremony need not have a formal reception line. With a long guest list, the receiving line can take quite a while. A cocktail hour with passed hors d'oeuvres is one way to keep your guests occupied while they wait.

Stage the receiving line in an area where you won't block the traffic flow and where your guests will not be crowded into a small space. There is no one right way to line up for this event. Usually the line is led by the bride's parents, then the bride and groom, then the groom's parents, and then the attendants. Some couples include only the honor attendants or none at all. Another idea is to begin with the bride's father, then the groom's mother, the bride and groom, the bride's mother, and the groom's father. That way introductions are easily made along the way. Other circumstances, such as divorced parents, step-parents, and children of the bride and groom might also have to be considered. Be sensitive to any tensions that may exist in these situations.

The receiving line is also a chance for you to introduce each other and each other's parents to friends and relatives from "the other side." As you accept congratulatory hugs and kisses from your guests, thank them for coming. Introduce your spouse and parents to the guests they do not know, adding a bit of information, such as "These are my parents' next-door neighbors, Gina and Howard Smith."

Make petal cones, page 84, and your guests can toss the petals after your ceremony.

setting up the reception

A WELL-DESIGNED FLOOR PLAN, WITH DESIGNATED AREAS FOR ALL OF the focal points of the reception, will ensure easy traffic flow. Guests will find their seats with ease and move effortlessly from one area to the next, never pausing to consider how masterfully you've orchestrated the site setup.

FOCAL POINTS

List all of the focal points of the reception, and station them in different areas where guests can gather for a few moments without blocking traffic or causing congestion. These stations might include a gift table, a guest book table or lectern, a table for arranging seating cards, a wedding cake table, a punch table, an area with memorabilia and photos, the bar, buffet tables, and the dance floor. For obvious reasons, a few of these stations, such as the seating card table and guest book, are best placed near the entrance. To avoid congestion, consider placing separate guest book pages on each table (page 93). Setting up other stations—the punch table, the cake table, and the bar—deeper into the room draws your guests away from the doorway and disperses the crowd.

If the reception includes a dance, make sure there is plenty of room for dancing. Designate an area for the band or DJ to set up equipment and make sure their electrical requirements will be met. Discuss the acoustics with the site manager and the band or DJ.

Create personal accents for your reception with a handmade guest book, page 93 or a wine glass votive, page 85.

ARRANGING THE TABLES

A full-meal reception should have a seating plan, whether it is served seated or buffet-style. Your guests will appreciate the effort you have taken to consider them individually. If the reception site is responsible for setting up the tables, request a diagram of the reception room setup from the site manager, so you will know how many tables to fill, how many guests will be seated at each table, and how the tables will be arranged.

For receptions held at sites where tables and chairs are not provided, you will need to find a rental company and make a thorough list of all the items you'll need. Rental companies have round and rectangular tables in many sizes, usually with inexpensive plywood tops that must be covered with tablecloths. Of course, the table linens can be rented as well. Round tables offer the most efficient seating. The chart opposite shows common sizes of tables, the number of people each will seat comfortably, and the tablecloth sizes required. This is based on the estimate that each place setting uses a space 24" (61 cm) wide and 18" (46 cm) deep. Allow 18" (46 cm) for chair depth and another 24" (61 cm) of moving space behind chairs. With this in mind, round tables that are set up so the chairs mesh like gear cogs can often seat more people than rectangular tables in the same space. Draw the reception area to scale on graph paper, including the guest table, head table, and all the focal point stations.

seating chart guidelines

The bride and groom are seated in the center of the head table, facing the guests, with the bride to the groom's right. The maid of honor sits on the groom's left; the best man sits on the bride's right. The other bridesmaids and groomsmen are seated in alternating sequence to the ends of the table. The flower girl and ring bearer sit with their parents. If the wedding party is small, the head table can include the spouses of the attendants, parents, and the officiant and spouse.

The parents of the bride and groom are seated at separate tables near the head table with grandparents and other close relatives or friends. The officiant and spouse, if not at the head table, are usually seated at the bride's parents' table. If parents have been divorced, they are usually seated at separate tables with their own circles of friends and relatives.

An alternative is to seat all the parents, grandparents, officiant, and spouse or other honored guest at one table, with the bride's mother and father across from each other. The groom's father sits at the bride's mother's right side, the officiant on her left. The groom's mother sits at the bride's father's right side, the officiant's spouse or other honored guest at his left.

Try to create a compatible group of friends and relatives of both the bride and groom at each table. Or fill tables with guests from one side, but intersperse the tables to encourage mixing.

Make place cards for everyone attending, writing their names on both the front and back, so they can be read by other guests around the table. If guests will pick up their place cards at the entrance, also write the table number on each card.

Arrange place cards in order by table, if they will be placed on the tables. Then make a large chart for display at the reception entrance to help guests find their seats. Or arrange place cards in alphabetical order if they will be lined up on a table at the reception entrance for your guests to pick up.

If place cards will be set on the tables, give a copy of the chart to the people who will set up the tables. Even if the catering service is not doing set-up, give them a copy, along with any notes for special dietary considerations of certain guests (arranged ahead of time).

TABLE SIZE	SEATS	SHORT TABLECLOTH	FLOORLENGTH CLOTH
36" (91.5 cm) round	4 to 5	60" (152.5 cm)	94" (239 cm)
48" (122 cm) round	6 to 8	70" (178 cm)	108" (275 cm)
60" (152.5 cm) round	8 to 10	84" (213.5 cm)	120" (305 cm)
72" (183 cm) round	10 to 12	90" (229 cm)	132" (335 cm)
36" (91.5 cm) square	4	52" (132 cm) square	
30" × 48" (76 × 122 cm)	4 to 6	52" × 70" (132 × 178 cm)	For floorlength cloths on
30" × 60" (76 × 152.5 cm)	6	60" × 84" (152.5 × 213.5 cm)	rectangular tables,
36" × 60" (91.5 × 152.5 cm)	6 to 8	60" × 84" (152.5 × 213.5 cm)	secure skirting to short
30" × 72" (76 × 183 cm)	6 to 8	60" × 84" (152.5 × 213.5 cm)	tablecloths.
40" × 72" (102 × 183 cm)	8	60" × 84" (152.5 × 213.5 cm)	
30" × 96" (76 × 244 cm)	8 to 10	60" × 120" (152.5 × 305 cm)	
40" × 96" (102 × 244 cm)	12	60" × 120" (152.5 × 305 cm)	
48" × 108" (122 × 275 cm)	12 to 14	60" × 120" (152.5 × 305 cm)	

decorations and favors

WHEN YOU START TO PLAN DECORATIONS, ENVISION YOUR RECEPTION site full of people dressed up for the occasion. You and your attendants will be dressed in your gowns and formalwear, carrying fresh-flower bouquets or wearing boutonnieres. The wedding cake will decorate a table in one area and beautifully wrapped gifts will occupy another. Now imagine additional ways to dress up the site without overshadowing these naturally decorative elements.

If your reception site regularly caters to weddings, they may have some decorations available for your use, such as mirror tiles for the centers of the tables, vases, hurricanes or candlesticks, potted plants, etc. It is important to check with the site manager about any restrictions they may have concerning decorations before you make any big plans. It would be a shame to blow the reception budget on hundreds of yards of tulle and twinkle lights to drape from the ceiling only to find out the reception site won't allow it. Find out when you will have access to the site for decorating, preferably after the tables are set but long enough ahead of time to allow decorators to attend the ceremony.

Make pretty grapevine chair wreaths for the back of the bride's and groom's chairs, page 86.

WHO'S GOING TO DECORATE?

Scale your decorating plans to fit the answer to this all-important question. You and your parents and attendants will be quite busy on the day of the wedding, so that means delegating (begging) someone else to do it. Sometimes the catering company or reception site workers will set up the tables with tablecloths, napkins, flatware and glassware, though you may have to make special arrangements at additional cost if you want the napkins folded a certain way or if you want wedding favors and place cards set out, too. If your florist is not supplying centerpieces, you'll have to trust that job to someone else, so centerpieces made ahead of time are a great idea. Of course, you always have the option of hiring a professional decorating service, if your budget will allow.

TABLE SURFACES

Because of the amount of space they occupy, the guests' tables can make a powerful decorating statement. A room full of cloth-covered tables decked out with fancy folded napkins in colors that echo the wedding scheme is an impressive sight. Shiny silverware and sparkling crystal glassware add exciting accents. Simple, elegant centerpieces and perhaps a scattering of colorful favors are all that is needed to make the table scape a feast for the eyes.

Keep centerpieces below eye level so that guests can easily converse across the table. While fresh floral centerpieces always add a touch of luxury, they may also strain the wedding budget, especially if they are provided by a florist. Small garden-flower arrangements or single blooms in bud vases are less costly, and you can amplify their effect for an evening wedding with the addition of romantic candles. A garland of silk flowers or greenery wrapped around the base of a hurricane candle is another quick and easy idea. Mirror tiles placed under the centerpieces double their size visually.

In a more casual approach, many couples choose to express favorite pastimes or seasonal themes in their centerpieces. Avid gardeners, for instance, might make centerpieces from clay pots, hand tools, and seed packets, inviting guests to plant the seeds as a memento. Campers could pitch a miniature tent in a bed of wheat grass in the center of each table. Baskets of colorful gourds make lovely low-cost autumn centerpieces. Clear glass balls nestled in tinsel fit a holiday theme. Double-duty centerpieces, such as a decorative container that holds a special favor for each guest at the table, are also a clever idea. Small wedding cakes, large enough to feed the guests at each table, along with a stack of dessert plates and a cake knife, invite guests to help themselves while serving as decorative features throughout the meal. A little imagination can spark some very creative ideas.

ADDITIONAL DÉCOR

Lighting has a great affect on the overall appearance and mood of the reception site. For romance and elegance, nothing beats the soft flickering glow of candlelight. Check that the room lighting can be turned down low enough to take advantage of candlelight but not so low that your guests have difficulty watching the reception events unfold. Avoid scented candles which can trigger allergies and sensitivities and compete with the smell and taste of the reception food.

Tulle is a light, airy netting, much like the netting of your veil, that gives a heavenly, cloud-like appearance when draped around special tables, over chairs at the head table, in doorways, around pillars, or over arbors. It is inexpensive and also looks great wrapped around strings of tiny twinkle lights. Just be sure to tape cords to the floor if they must span an area where people will be walking.

Ribbons, used as streamers or tied up in bows, add colorful accents to special tables and chair backs. Leave long, luxurious tails, especially if the reception is held outdoors where they can flutter in the breeze. For the sake of economy, buy craft ribbon by the bolt at a craft store or discount center, rather than by the yard from a fabric store.

Create your own favors, page 90, or your own centerpieces, page 88.

If your reception style is more casual, balloons and crepe paper streamers may do the trick. Also consider theme oriented decorations and favors. If held outdoors, your reception could be decorated in the style of a Hawaiian luau and you could treat your guests to pretty shells or small bottles of sunscreen. Outdoor locations may not need extra decorating, especially if there are already pretty flowers and vegetation all around.

FAVORS

Favors, if you decide to give them, should appeal to all of your guests. A sweet treat always fits the bill. It's also nice to tie the favor to the wedding theme or give something that has personal significance to the bride and groom. Candy or petits fours can be personalized with unique wrappers that carry a note of thanks from the bride and groom. Ornaments or candy canes given out near the holidays, flower bulbs in the fall, seed packets in the spring, or visors or fans for an outdoor summer wedding are sure to please the majority of your guests. You might consider giving special favors for children, such as yo-yos, Slinkies, coloring books and crayons, or little stuffed animals. Some couples opt not to give favors and use the money to make a donation to their favorite charity instead.

schedule of events

MORE THAN A JOYOUS CELEBRATION, YOUR RECEPTION MAY FEATURE several events that follow tradition and keep your guests entertained. As an organizing framework, a schedule of events also keeps the party rolling in a planned sequence.

As the happy couple, you choose which elements to include and which to ignore. There may also be some significant family or cultural rituals that you want to add to your celebration. Your choices may depend on the time of day and style of reception as well as your preferences. You may feel, for instance, that the tossing of the garter is a bit too garish for your sophisticated champagne brunch. If your marriage joins two people from different cultural backgrounds, you might choose to highlight the reception with traditions that pay tribute to both.

EXTRAS

Throughout the reception you may choose to include entertaining readings or vocal performances by special guests. Many couples present a slide show or video montage of their separate lives, their meeting, and their courtship. The reception could begin or end with a grand march, led by the bride and groom and their attendants. If the couple did not receive a rice, bubble, or flower petal shower after the ceremony, this ritual could be staged as the couple leaves the reception.

When you have drawn up your schedule of reception events, with the approximate times at which each should take place, delegate someone to initiate the events. This could be the couple you have asked to help host the occasion, a wedding day coordinator, the caterer, or the band leader or DJ. While you are entertaining your guests and enjoying the celebration, someone else can worry about the schedule.

food and beverages

THE LARGEST SLICE OF THE WEDDING BUDGET PIE usually goes to the reception food and beverages. With careful planning, some wise decisions, and a little creativity, you can stay within your budget while treating your guests to some fabulous hospitality.

FINDING A CATERER

Once you have determined your budget, made the big decisions about the style and location of your wedding, and estimated the number of guests, it's time to shop for and book a caterer. If you are holding your reception at a hotel, country club, or special-event facility, chances are they have their own in-house catering

reception events schedule

COCKTAIL HOUR As a kickoff to your reception, the cocktail hour may last an hour to an hour and a half. Often the wedding party is caught up in a photo shoot after the ceremony and unable to get to the reception before the guests arrive, so the cocktail hour keeps the guests entertained.

RECEIVING LINE This gives the bride and groom a chance to thank everyone for coming and gives each guest an opportunity to congratulate the newlyweds. More details are given on page 47.

SEATING OF GUESTS At a dinner reception, this signals the end of the cocktail hour in anticipation of the meal to be served soon. As the wedding party takes their seats at the head table, guests will follow suit at the urging of the reception hosts or caterer.

CHAMPAGNE TOASTS Traditionally the best man gives the first toast. This can take place after everyone has been seated for a formal dinner reception or as the first course is being served. If the meal is served buffet-style, ideally toasting should take place before guests begin to line up. At a reception where a full meal is not served, the best man can offer the first toast soon after all the guests have passed through the receiving line. The maid of honor traditionally gives the second toast. The groom responds with a welcoming, thanking, speech to his guests and a tribute to his new bride. The bride may also offer a speech of her own. At some time during the meal or shortly after the first toasts, the father of the bride and father of the groom may also offer their toasts. Other guests who are especially close to the bride and groom may get into the act as well. Don't forget the key ingredient—the champagne. Before the toasts begin, make arrangements for your guests to be served a glass by wait staff going around to all the tables or walking among the guests with trays.

DINNER The bride and groom are served first, then the attendants and others at the head table. Parents' tables follow them, and then the rest of the guests are served. If the meal is served buffet-style, someone should be assigned to usher the guests to the buffet line, table by table. More information on meal service can be found on page 54.

CAKE CUTTING In a formal ritual, the bride and groom cut and serve each other the first piece of cake (page 58). Then parents are served, followed by the rest of the guests. Coffee service should begin at the same time. This can take place after all the guests have finished the main meal and before the wedding dance begins. If there is no dance, the cake cutting usually takes place about an hour before the end of the reception, as a signal that the party is winding down.

FIRST DANCE The bride and groom traditionally dance the first dance together to a tune that has special meaning for them. After a while they split up and the groom dances with his mother while the bride dances with her father. Other pairings may have the groom dancing with the bride's mother while the bride dances with the groom's father; the best man dances with the bride while the maid of honor dances with the groom. Then everyone else is invited to join them on the dance floor.

DOLLAR DANCE Guests pay a dollar apiece to take a spin around the dance floor with the bride or the groom. In some traditions, the guests pin dollar bills to the bride's skirt hem. In another scenario, the best man and maid of honor collect the money.

GARTER TOSS Near the end of the reception, the bride sits in a chair while the single men gather around. The groom removes the garter from her right leg and tosses it to the waiting crowd. Legend has it that the man who catches it will be the next to wed.

BOUQUET TOSS The single women gather around and the bride tosses her bouquet (or one made just for this ritual) over her back toward them. If the superstition holds true, the woman who catches the bouquet will be the next to wed. In some traditions the man who caught the garter then dances with the woman who caught the bouquet.

Combine your
centerpiece with
your beverage
service for dinner,
page 87.

and beverage service. It's also a good bet that they strongly discourage or forbid outside catering or will ask you to stick to one of the caterers on their preferred list if they don't offer the service. By choosing an all-purpose facility you won't have to shop for separate vendors, make arrangements for them to gain access to the site, and coordinate all of their efforts. Possible disadvantages could be hidden costs and charges for services that you don't really want. The interview forms on page 116 and 119 will help you ask the right questions when you shop for catering and beverage service.

Caterers charge on a per-guest basis. Once you know how many guests you will have and your budget for food, do the math and figure out how much you can afford to spend. With this information, the caterer will be able to give you an idea of the kind of food and the style of service they can offer at that price. If you find that your ideas don't match up with reality, you have two alternatives — settle for less expensive food and service style or cut back on your guest list.

If your reception site doesn't offer catering, talk to friends who have recently married and ask their advice. When you interview caterers, get at least three references and follow up on them. Ask each couple how many guests were at their wedding and where it was held. Find out what was served and what style of service was used. Ask if the food was tasty, attractively presented, and served at the right temperature. Also ask questions about the efficiency and professionalism of the wait staff. It may be out of line for you to ask friends how much they paid, but you can ask if there were any hidden costs in their bill. By all means, make sure the caterer is licensed and check credentials with the better business bureau.

STYLES OF SERVICE

There are several ways of serving food to your guests. The style you choose is not as dependent on the wedding formality as it is on the number of guests to be served, the logistics involved, the type of meal being served, and the cost.

One option is to have guests seated and served a full meal, course by course, by a wait staff. It is a good idea to specify the seating arrangement with this type of service. Not only does it offer the guests the convenience of not having to scramble to find a seat, it also makes it easier for the caterer to accommodate guests who have special dietary needs. Plus, if you want to offer a choice of entrées, which you would include on the invitation response cards, you can chart out for the wait staff which entrée goes to each guest. Seated, also called sit-down, meals can be served in one of three ways: plated, Russian, or French. In plated service, the food is arranged on plates in equal portions in the kitchen and then brought into the dining room and served to each guest. For Russian service, the plates are already at the table when the guests are seated. The wait staff serves courses from platters that they bring around to the tables; usually one waiter is assigned each course. French service is similar, except that one waiter holds the the platter while another serves the food.

Serving the food from one long buffet or several buffet stations is less expensive than sit-down style because it requires a smaller wait staff. Though not absolutely necessary, it is still a thoughtful gesture on your part to assign seats. Flatware, glassware, and napkins are placed at the tables before the reception begins. Guests are ushered table by table to the buffet line and return to their assigned seat. If seats are not assigned and guests are free to find a place to sit (as may be the case for a small house reception) plates, flatware, napkins, and beverage glasses are picked up at the buffet. To lessen the need for juggling, wait staff can bring beverages to the tables.

Buffet meals can be self-serve, allowing guests to choose the foods and portions they want. Or, servers can stand behind the buffet table and serve equal portions to the guests. Sometimes a combination of styles is appropriate, such as having a server slice and serve roast beef while the guests help themselves for the rest of the meal.

Setting up separate buffet stations for appetizers, salads, main course dishes, desserts, and beverages keeps traffic flowing smoothly and encourages guests to eat at their own pace. It also gives you the opportunity to serve some unique foods, such as made-to-order crepes or omelettes, sushi, fajitas, or gourmet coffee drinks.

If you will not be serving a full meal, or if you want to serve hors d'oeuvres during the cocktail hour, passed-tray service is a stylish way to do it. Wait staff circulates around the room with trays of various finger-food appetizers or desserts for your guests. This is also a smart way to serve champagne. Passed-tray service can be accompanied by a buffet station where you might also offer foods that need to be plated and eaten with utensils.

WHAT WILL YOU SERVE?

You have probably decided, according to the time of day, what type of meal to serve. If you are not planning a dance, breakfast, brunch, or lunch can follow a morning wedding; early afternoon weddings may be followed by cocktails and hors d'oeuvres or dessert receptions. A late afternoon wedding should be followed by a full dinner.

The food you serve is your way of thanking your guests for coming to your wedding. Ideally, it should be a statement about your personal style, too, so serve them your favorites. If you've settled on a theme for your wedding, select foods that fit. For instance, individual boxed lunches from the local deli accompanied by a fruit and melon buffet would fit a casual outdoor wedding and reception in the park. You might select foods that support an ethnic theme or reflect your cultural background. Also consider featuring seasonal or holiday favorites to fit the time of year.

BEVERAGE SERVICE

If you will be serving alcohol at your reception, you have several decisions to make: what kind of alcohol to serve, how and when to serve it, and how much you can afford.

You have lots of options. If the facility offers regular bar service, your guests can purchase whatever they want. If you will be purchasing the alcohol, you can stock a full bar or limit the choices to beer and wine only, in which case, you have the option of purchasing beer by the keg or by the bottle. You may be able to offer more variety with bottled beer, including non-alcohol varieties. Bottled beer is usually more expensive than keg beer unless a full keg is tapped near the end of the evening and barely used. Three kinds of wine are usually served: red (Cabernet Sauvignon), rosé (white Zinfandel), and white (Chardonnay). Champagne or sparkling wine may be served for toasting the bride and groom, or you may decide to have a champagne-only reception. Whether or not you serve alcohol, you should have plenty of soft drinks, bottled water, and coffee.

Whether or not you serve alcohol, you should have plenty of soft drinks, bottled water, and coffee.

HOW TO SERVE IT

Reception sites, such as hotels and private clubs, usually offer complete beverage service. This means your guests can purchase drinks at the bar; the facility profits from every drink sold. You can designate an hour or so as open bar, during which you pick up the tab for the drinks. Or, if money is no object, you can may offer to pick up the tab for the entire evening. Additional costs to you may include wine with dinner and champagne for toasting, both served by the caterer's wait staff. Sometimes the facility will allow you to purchase your own alcohol and they will serve it for a corkage fee. This can save you a lot of money, especially if you purchase the alcohol at wholesale cost. You can also return unopened bottles. If the site doesn't have beverage service, you will need to find a caterer who is licensed to serve alcohol or you may have to obtain a one-day special event liquor license, purchase your own alcohol, and hire your own bartenders. Check your local ordinances.

How much can you afford? Make your final decisions about beverage service after you have planned the other major reception expenses. One bottle of wine contains about six servings. One bottle (750 mL) of hard liquor makes about 20 drinks. A safe level of alcohol consumption is one drink per hour, though many guests will drink more than that. Younger guests tend to consume more than older guests. The more relaxed the atmosphere and the longer the event, the more alcohol will be consumed. Wedding dances are often accompanied by bar service all evening, but closing the bar an hour before the end of the reception and offering soft drinks is a good idea. As hosts, you are liable for the safety of your guests.

wedding cake

how can we save money on the cake?

Bakers suggest that you order cake for 75 percent of your guests, since not everyone will eat cake.

If you are planning other desserts as well, order cake for half of your guests.

If your guest list is large, you can have a modest wedding cake for display with less expensive sheet cakes for serving the guests.

Sometimes the wedding cake itself is made of decorated Styrofoam layers except for the top layer. After the bride and groom cut into the top layer, the guests are served from sheet cakes kept in the kitchen.

ALONG WITH THE BRIDAL GOWN AND FLOWERS, YOUR WEDDING CAKE is one of the main focal points of your wedding. It deserves careful planning and selection and a well-staged area at the reception for showing it off.

You want your wedding cake to be delicious and beautiful and to reflect the theme of your wedding. Most cake designers suggest that you select your cake after you have booked your reception site and ordered the bride's gown, bridesmaids' dresses, and flowers. Given all of this information, the cake designer can design a cake that fits the formality of your wedding, repeating design elements used in the dresses or making frosting flowers that resemble flowers in your bouquet. By this time, you should also have a fairly accurate guest count, which directly affects the size of cake to buy and ultimately the price you will pay.

FINDING A CAKE DESIGNER

Talk to friends who have recently been married and other wedding professionals, such as your photographer and florist. Your reception site or caterer may include the wedding cake as a part of their package. If you are happy with the choices and prices they offer, you may not need to look elsewhere. An advantage to having the cake included in the reception site and/or catering package is that you do not have to make other arrangements for delivery and set-up or for returning foundation platforms and supports. However, you should be free to look elsewhere if you wish. Often, reception sites and caterers outsource the wedding cake anyway, and you may find that prices are not much different. The bakery interview form on page 118 will help you interview prospective cake designers.

PRICE

Wedding cakes are usually priced by the slice or by the number of guests they will serve. Depending on the type of frosting used, the intricacy of the design, and the flavor and filling, you can expect price variations from $1.50 to $15.00 per slice. Reception sites and caterers may tack on a per-serving cutting fee if the cake was delivered from an outside baker. Prepare yourself for sticker shock if you have found a gorgeous cake in a magazine that you want your designer to duplicate. Many cakes pictured in magazines are considered "couture" cakes and are very difficult and thus expensive to make.

DISPLAYING THE CAKE

As an important focal point of your reception, the wedding cake should be displayed on its own table in a well-lit, low-traffic area of the reception site. Pay close attention to the walls behind the cake and arrange a backdrop, if necessary to cover up distracting wall hangings or wallpaper. Remember that several photos will be taken of the cake. Make sure the table itself is sturdy and the legs are locked in place. The table can be draped in fabric with an overskirt of netting drawn up in swags and secured with fresh or silk flowers.

cake terms to know

BASKETWEAVE This technique for piping frosting onto the cake surface features interwoven vertical and horizontal lines that look like a wicker basket.

BUTTERCREAM The most popular kind of frosting, buttercream is smooth and creamy and it stays soft so it is easy to cut through. It is easily colored and flavored and works very well for piping designs onto the cake or for flavoring between layers. Because it is made with real butter, it will melt in hot weather.

FILLING This is the yummy stuff sandwiched between the layers of your cake. It could be as simple as buttercream icing or you might select a fruity jelly-type filling or something made with cream cheese or whipped cream.

FONDANT This sweet, elastic icing is made of sugar, corn syrup, and gelatin that is rolled out much like a pie crust and then draped over the cake. Seams are sealed and smoothed to a porcelain finish. Fondant icing is more labor-intensive than buttercream, so the cost is higher.

GANACHE This sweet, rich chocolate can be used as an icing or filling. Its texture is somewhere between that of fudge and mousse. With cream as one of its ingredients, ganache will soften and melt in heat and humidity.

GUM PASTE This edible paste of sugar, gelatin, and cornstarch is used to mold realistic fruits and flowers to decorate the cake.

MARZIPAN This edible (and very delicious) paste made of ground almonds, sugar, and egg whites is used to mold objects like flowers and fruit to decorate the cake. Marzipan can also be rolled out like fondant icing and used to cover the cake entirely.

PILLARS Supports made of plastic or wood are used to separate the layers of a tiered cake.

PIPING Icing is loaded into a pastry bag fitted with a metal tip and squeezed out through the tip to create design details. Depending on the tip used and the movement of the hands, the icing can be shaped into dots, lines, leaves, flowers, basket-weave patterns, and other designs.

ROYAL ICING This icing, made from egg whites and powdered sugar, is piped out into designs or flowers that become hard and brittle when they dry.

TOPPERS

Traditionally objects like bride and groom figurines, wedding bells, hearts, or lovebirds have been placed on top of the cake. More often now, couples are choosing to top their cakes with fresh flowers, frosting flowers, or bows. If you use fresh flowers, make sure they are not poisonous and are pesticide-free. A good idea is to have a small floral arrangement made in a plastic container that sits on top of the cake.

THE CAKE CUTTING CEREMONY

The bride and groom together cut and eat the first slice of cake, symbolizing their desire to love and nurture each other. The bride takes the cake knife in her right hand and the groom places his right hand over hers. After cutting a small wedge from the bottom layer and placing it on a plate, the groom feeds the bride the first bite and then she feeds the groom. Slices are then cut for the parents, and the bride and groom deliver cake to their new inlaws. Following the ceremony, the caterer cuts cake for the guests.

ANNIVERSARY LAYER

The top layer of the cake is traditionally saved to be eaten at the first anniversary. Though it probably won't taste as good as it did on your wedding day, the best way to preserve it is to wrap it airtight in several layers of plastic before freezing it. This is one of those duties you will want to delegate to someone else.

reception music

The music is really intended to entertain your guests, so consider their ages and musical preferences along with your own.

NOTHING SETS THE TONE OF A RECEPTION LIKE THE MUSIC. WHETHER it serves as a gentle background to conversation and cocktails or stirs the crowd into lively dancing, music is the key entertainment ingredient. Different kinds of music suit different event styles. The formality of the reception, the location, the schedule of events you have planned, and even the time of day can have an impact on the kind of music you select and how it is performed. Of course, money considerations enter into the plans as well, but the music usually takes a smaller bite out of the budget than other elements of the reception. In order to determine the right kind of music for your reception, decide what you want the music to do and what mood or theme you want the music to support.

BACKGROUND ENTERTAINMENT

Music needs to suit the size of the space. A small reception hall in a church probably calls for a pianist perhaps with a flute. An outdoor venue, where the acoustics aren't much help, can use more musicians or a good sound system. A larger facility can accommodate a larger band.

Consider what your guests will be doing while the music is playing. If they will be mingling and conversing, enjoying cocktails and hors d'oeuvres, the music should be soft. Consider a harpist or a small string orchestra. If you want the music to be a focal point, with the guests gathered around to listen and watch, consider hiring a swing band or a brass quintet.

What type of music will create the right mood for your reception? If you are envisioning a formal, high-style affair, your choices might be piano, woodwinds, or strings playing classical, romantic music. Maybe your taste tends more toward a jazz band or pop orchestra.

If you imagine a less formal, jubilant atmosphere, maybe a mariachi band with guitars and trumpets are a better fit.

DANCE MUSIC

If your reception includes a dance, you can hire either a live band or a DJ. Depending on the area where you live, you are likely to find a wide range of options and prices in each category, though DJs are usually less expensive. Bands range in size and vary by the instruments they play. Some include vocalists while others are strictly instrumental. DJ companies offer services that range from a single DJ to a DJ accompanied by an entertaining master of ceremonies, costumed dancers, and a laser light show. It is important to listen to tapes of the musicians you are considering, but even more helpful if you can see and hear them in action. Forms for interviewing and auditioning musicians are on page 126. As with hiring of any professional service, be sure to get references and follow up on them. If you have booked one of the more popular wedding reception facilities in your area, the site manager may be a good source for band or DJ suggestions. Good dance bands and DJs are booked up to a year in advance, so start shopping as soon as you have made the big decisions about location and time. There is plenty of time later to decide on the exact play list, as long as you choose a band or DJ with a wide repertoire.

The music is really intended to entertain your guests, so consider their ages and musical preferences along with your own. When you mix different styles of music throughout the evening, you are more likely to please all ages and to get more people out on the dance floor. The more people you can get out on the dance floor, the more fun everyone will have (including the wallflowers), and ultimately the more successful the reception will be.

A seasoned DJ or band leader with lots of wedding experience often acts as a master of ceremonies, cuing the reception events. Provided with a list of the songs you want played for different times during the evening, this person will announce your cake-cutting, your first dance, and other special moments you have planned. In fact, an emcee who can develop a friendly rapport with the audience can turn an average reception into a fabulous party. Go over your schedule of reception events (page 115) and make a list of different songs that could be played for each. There are lots of suggestions on web sites and the musicians themselves can offer ideas. Choose songs that have particular meaning for you. Then make sure that the band or DJ you select can play them.

Along with the schedule of events, you should provide your musicians with a play list. This doesn't mean that you need to plan out four hours of music (50 to 60 tunes); that's part of their job. But you should provide a list of songs you definitely want them to play and a list of songs or styles you don't want them to play. (Keep in mind that, even if you hate The Electric Slide or the Beer Barrel Polka, they are both tunes that are almost guaranteed to get people on the dance floor!)

how can we keep the reception music within our budget?

Consider hiring some musicians from a local college or music school to play during your reception.

wedding crafts

INDIVIDUALITY IS AN ESSENTIAL INGREDIENT of the perfect wedding. Handcrafted items like a ring bearer pillow, flower girl basket, keepsake wedding card box, or a unity candle are unique accents to your wedding day and also become cherished mementos. Crafting gives you countless options for colors and designs, while easing the budget and reserving more money for things like food and entertainment. Handmade invitations are more affordable than purchased ones, and they give your guests a glimpse of the truly personal event you have in store. Making your own headpiece and veil is far easier than you might imagine, and the cost savings can be tremendous compared to an identical set bought at a bridal salon. No one expects the bride to do it all. In fact, friends and family members who love to sew, craft, or arrange flowers would be honored if you asked them to make an item for your wedding as their gift to you. What could add more meaning to your special day than beautiful accessories crafted with care, love, and personal style!

vellum-wrapped invitation

BLANK INVITATIONS, ENCLOSURE CARDS, AND envelopes are available in a variety of styles, making it easy for you to simply print your own invitations on your computer. The kits come with instructions for setting up a document in basic publishing software on your home computer. The vellum wrap with pressure embossed initials, shown at left, adds a dressy, personal touch.

1 Place the invitation diagonally on the pattern paper. Trace around the outer edges. Using a straightedge, extend the side, top, and bottom lines to the edges of the pattern paper. The side lines become fold guidelines. Round off the side extensions, using a dinner plate for a guide. Cut out the pattern.

2 Trace the pattern onto vellum. Mark the top and bottom of the foldlines, and score them, using a straightedge and stylus. Cut out the wrap, using scissors with decorative-edge blades.

3 Cut slits the width of the ribbon in the center of the foldlines. Fold in the flaps. Mark a small dot on each flap in the center of the overlap. Punch holes at the marks.

4 Emboss the bride's and groom's initials or a favorite design on each flap, using an embossing plate and stylus.

5 Thread the ribbon from the outside through the hole of the left flap, through the fold slit, across the outside back, through the other fold slit, and out the right flap hole. Insert the printed invitation. As you fold in the flaps, thread the ribbon from the right flap through the hole of the left flap, and tie a bow.

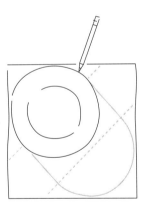

STEP 1

materials

Invitation kit

Computer with basic publishing software; printer

12" × 12" (30.5 × 30.5 cm) sheet of vellum, one per invitation

12" × 12" (30.5 × 30.5 cm) sheet of paper for pattern

Straightedge

Scissors

Scissors with decorative-edge blades

Small hole punch

Craft knife

Narrow, sheer ribbon, about 3/4 yd. (0.7 m) per invitation

Ball-tip stylus

Embossing plates with initials of the couple or other design

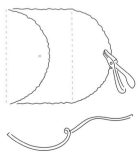

STEP 3

photo invitation

MANY COUPLES PREFER A MORE INFORMAL WEDDING, beginning with their invitation. This square invitation features a small snapshot of the bride and groom creatively veiled by the wedding message printed on sheer vellum. The corner flaps of the invitation are tied in place by a ribbon threaded through a stamped embossed seal tag.

1   Cut an 8" (20.5 cm) square of card stock for the invitation base. Mark a point ¼" (6 mm) from the edge at the center of each side. Using a metal straightedge and a craft knife turned with the blade facing up, score lines connecting the marks to the outer edges. Trim away the small triangles at the side centers.

2   Create a letter-size document in landscape position, using publishing software. Create a 5" (12.7 cm) square text box. Place guide lines to block off a section about ½" (1.3 cm) larger than the photo. Type your wedding invitation message, leaving room for the photo. Copy the box so you can print two per page. Print out the message on sheer vellum. Cut them out, 5" (12.7 cm) square.

3   Cut a rectangle of contrasting card stock ¼" (6 mm) larger than the photo. Secure the photo to the center of the rectangle, using glue or tape tabs. Secure the backed photo to the inside of the invitation base, where it will show through the reserved space on the message. Secure the sheer message to the center of the base, over the photo, using vellum tape in the upper corners.

4   Stamp and emboss a design onto the contrasting card stock to make a seal tag; cut out. Punch a small hole in the center.

5   Cut two small slits about ¼" (6 mm) apart in the centers of the top and bottom flaps. Fold in the side flaps, then the bottom and top. Wrap ribbon around the card and through the slits, then poke both ends through the hole in the seal tag. Tie in a bow.

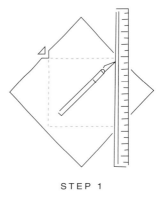

STEP 1

materials

8½" × 11" (21.8 × 28 cm) card stock

Contrasting card stock for photo back and seal tag

5½" (14 cm) square envelope

Printable sheer vellum

Computer with basic publishing software; printer

Paper cutter

Metal ruler

Craft knife

Snapshot of the bride and groom, about 1½" (3.8 cm) square

Glue stick or tape tabs; vellum tape

Rubber stamp design; ink, embossing powder, and heat gun

Small hole punch

Ribbon

thank-you notes

LIKE THE INVITATIONS, YOUR THANK-YOU NOTES can be formal or casual, traditional or contemporary. Blank note cards with matching envelopes can be embellished to reflect the style of your wedding or you can create unique personal thank-you notes using your computer and printer.

materials

FORMAL

Blank note cards with matching envelopes

Sheer, colored, patterned vellum

"Thank You" rubber stamp

Embossing ink, powder, and heat gun

Vellum tape

Scissors

Scissors with deckle-edge blades

Small paper punch

Narrow ribbon

CASUAL

8½" x 11" (21.8 × 28 cm) card stock

Matching envelopes

Computer with basic publishing software; printer

Metal straightedge

Craft knife and cutting mat or paper cutter

FORMAL THANK-YOU CARD

1   Cut the vellum slightly smaller than the front of the note card; trim the sides and bottom with deckle-blade scissors.

2   Stamp and emboss "Thank You" in the center of the vellum. Secure the top of the vellum to the top of the card, using vellum tape.

3   Punch holes through the vellum and card front, about 1" (2.5 cm) from the outer edges. Thread ribbon through the holes and tie in a bow.

4   Cut a rectangle of vellum slightly smaller than the envelope. Trim the upper edge with deckle scissors. Slip the vellum into the envelope; secure along the upper edge, using vellum tape.

CASUAL THANK-YOU CARD

1   Create a letter-size document in landscape position. Place a text box in the lower half of the document. Type the message "(Bride's name) and (Groom's name) thank you!" several times. Use a bold font for the names, and change the fonts of the other words so that no two sentences look alike. Then copy and paste the text repeatedly until the entire text box is filled.

2   Print the card stock. You will be able to get two cards per sheet. Score the sheet just above the first line of text; fold in half. Using a metal straightedge and craft knife or a paper cutter, cut the cards ¼" (6 mm) narrower and shorter than the envelopes.

materials

Two-color firm paper or lightweight card stock, one 8½" × 11" (21.8 × 28 cm) sheet per program

Computer with basic publishing software; printer

Straightedge and fine-point stylus or craft knife

Bone paper folder

2" (5 cm) square paper punch

2" (5 cm) round paper punch

Wedding ring trinkets (or similar items of your choice)

Ribbon

Hot-glue gun

ceremony program

WITH A COMPUTER, PRINTER, AND BASIC PUBLISHING SOFTWARE, YOU can produce ceremony programs that are sophisticated and professional with a personal touch. A trifold design provides six possible surfaces for placing text: three on the outside and three on the inside. Depending on how much information you wish to include, you can create a text box for each surface or choose to leave some of them blank. In the sample shown, the outer first flap announces the marriage, the inner flap cites the location and date, and the inner center panel is reserved for the order of the ceremony. One inner side panel can be used to list the ceremony participants. On the other side, you may want to include text for a group prayer, a poem or other reading, or your personal message of love and gratitude.

Select a firm paper that can be run through your printer. A lightweight card stock that has coordinating colors on opposite sides will accent the framed cutouts on the program flaps.

1   Create a letter-size document in landscape position, using publishing software. Set up guide lines dividing the document vertically into three equal parts. Set up a horizontal guide line 3" (7.5 cm) from the top of the document. Center a 3" × 5" (7.5 × 12.7 cm) text box in each lower section. Save the document once as the program outside and again as the program inside.

2   On outside of the program, type the marriage announcement in the desired font and size in the right-hand text box. Type the location and date in the upper part of the left-hand text box.

3   On the inside of the program, type the ceremony order in the center text box. If desired, type the names of the attendants and ceremony participants in the left-hand box; type a personal message, poem, or prayer in the right-hand box.

4   Print out the program, front and back, as a trial. Double-check the spelling, grammar, and spacing. Fold the paper to make sure the text boxes are properly arranged. Make any necessary changes. If changes have been made, run another trial. Print the programs.

5   Using a straightedge and a fine-point stylus or a craft knife turned with the blade facing up, score the inside of the program vertically 3⅝" (9.3 cm) from the right side; fold the right flap inward along the score, using a bone paper folder. Score the second foldline along the edge of the first flap; fold. This will allow the outer flap to extend slightly over the first fold. Fold a trial program into thirds to use as a guide for folding the programs. Using the guide, make pencil dots near the outer edges of the program inside at the folds. Fold in the right flap first; then the left flap.

6   Center the square 2" (5 cm) hole punch in the upper 3" (7.5 cm) of the right flap of the trial program. Punch the hole. Trace the square onto the inner flap. Center the round hole punch in the traced square; punch the round hole. Use the trial program as a guide when punching the holes in the programs.

7   Tie two wedding ring trinkets together with a short piece of ribbon. Apply a dot of hot glue to the back of the knot, and secure to the middle of the inside center section.

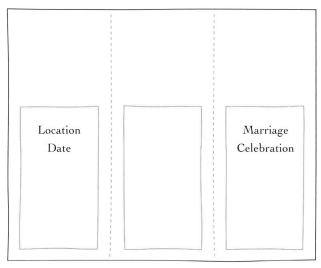

| Location Date | | Marriage Celebration |

STEP 2

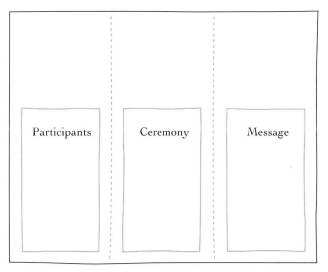

| Participants | Ceremony | Message |

STEP 3

headpiece and circle veil

MAKING YOUR OWN HEADPIECE AND VEIL CAN SAVE YOU $200 OR MORE, depending on its style and length. The materials—often better in quality than those used in ready-made veils—are all available in the bridal departments of major fabric stores or from internet supply sources. The techniques require little or no machine sewing, as most of the embellishments are glued in place.

The headpiece shown here is made from a bent band form that has been covered with horsehair net. Clusters of silk flowers, called sprays or falls, are simply glued to the form. The full-circle veil, attached at the back of the headpiece, falls in two curvy layers over the shoulders and arms to just below the waist. If desired, a narrow satin ribbon can be sewn around the outer edge of the veil to give it more definition.

CIRCLE VEIL

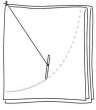

STEP 2

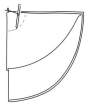

STEP 4

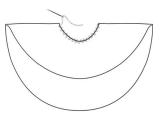

STEP 5

materials

HEADPIECE

Bent band headpiece form, covered with horsehair net

Silk flower sprays or falls, enough to cover the headpiece

Fabric glue

½ yd. (0.5 m) buttonhole looping

Bobby pins

6" (15 cm) soft, narrow hook and loop tape

CIRCLE VEIL

2 yd. (1.85 m) illusion netting in a color to match your dress

String, pushpin, and fabric marker, for drawing a circle

Hand needle and thread

6½ yd. (5.95 m) satin ribbon, ⅛" (3 mm) wide for veil edge trim, optional

HEADPIECE

1 Arrange the silk flower sprays or falls on the outer surface of the headpiece form so that the entire base is covered. Allow some of the items to extend over the side points; fill in any empty spaces with individual pieces. Pin the items in place, and try on the headpiece. Make any necessary adjustments. Glue the items in place using fabric glue. Allow to dry.

2 Cut a length of buttonhole looping slightly shorter than the headpiece front. Glue it to the underside of the frame, near the front, with the loops facing forward. These will be used to secure the headpiece to the hair with bobby pins.

3 Glue the loop side of the hook and loop tape to the center, underside of the frame back, near the outer edge. This will be used to hold the veil in place.

CIRCLE VEIL

1 Open the illusion and refold down the center, aligning the outer edges; fold again in the opposite direction, aligning four corners. Pin layers together to keep them from shifting.

2 Tie a long string to a pushpin and insert the pin into the work surface at the upper point of the folds. Tie the other end to a fabric marker 35" (89 cm) from the pin. Draw an arc on the illusion, keeping the marker upright and the string taut between the pushpin and the marker. Cut on the marked line to form a circle.

3 Unfold the veil illusion. Stitch a narrow ribbon about ½" (1.3 cm) from the outer edge, if desired. Use a straight stitch down the center of the ribbon, overlapping the ends as you finish. Carefully trim away all the excess veil illusion.

What is a bent band?

This headpiece shape begins as a circle that is bent on opposite sides and shaped to fit the head. It offers more fullness at the sides, flattering for a bride with a narrow face. Hair can be worn in an upsweep inside the opening when both bands are decorative. The veil is attached under the lower edge of the back band. Sometimes the back band is merely a bare support wire, which can be hidden under hair that is worn down, making it suitable for shorter hair styles. A veil can then be attached under the back edge of the front band. A plain back band can also be worn over the hair and used for attaching the veil.

4 Fold the top of the circle down 30" (76 cm). Fold the layers in half lengthwise. Retie the string to the marker 14" (35.5 cm) from the pushpin. Draw a smaller arc, and cut the illusion. Unfold the veil.

5 Fold the upper layer down aligning the top and bottom edges of the inner circle. Thread a needle with a double thread; knot the ends together. Beginning at one upper edge of the inner circle, take a stitch through both layers; secure the thread by running the needle between the threads before pulling the knot tight.

6 Stitch the layers together along the inner curve, taking 1/4" (6 mm) stitches that wrap around the cut edges, going about 1/4" (6 mm) deep into the edges. Work the needle in a spiral pattern, inserting from the back to the front; fill the needle with stitches before pulling the thread through. Repeat to the opposite side of the inner circle.

7 Pull up on the thread, gathering the veil edge to about 6" (15 cm); knot the thread. Stitch the veil to the lower edge of the hook tape, with the short side of the veil and the hook side of the tape facing up. Attach the veil to the headpiece by fastening the hook and loop tapes.

materials

9½" (24.3 cm)
of satin ribbon, 1½"
(3.8 cm) wide

2½" (6.5 cm) of ribbon,
⅜" (1 cm) wide

Lucky penny

STEP 1

penny pocket

A QUAINT SUPERSTITION SUGGESTS THAT THE
bride should wear a penny, minted in the year she gets
married, inside her shoe to bring her good luck. This
dainty little penny pocket will keep your good luck token
in place.

1   Fold the wide ribbon in half, right sides together. Stitch
the ends together in an arc. Trim close to the stitches. Turn
right side out, and press.

2   Turn the folded end up 1½" (3.8 cm), forming the
pocket. Place the narrow ribbon across the middle of the
pocket; tuck the ends between the layers. Stitch along the
pocket sides, catching the narrow ribbon.

3   Turn the stitched end down, forming a flap. Press. Tuck
the penny into the pocket, and close the flap, tucking it
under the narrow ribbon.

keepsake garter

materials

Sheer ribbon, 4" to 5" (10 to 12.7 cm) wide, long enough to go around your leg twice

Satin ribbon, 3/4" (2 cm) wide, enough to go around your leg twice plus extra for bow

Small piece of 1/8" (3 mm) ribbon

Elastic, 1/2" (1.3 cm) wide, enough to go around your leg plus 1" (2.5 cm)

Small safety pin or bodkin

Needle and thread

Something old

GARTERS ARE INEXPENSIVE AND SO QUICK TO make. Consider making two; one to toss and one to keep. This delicate sheer keepsake garter is made from ribbons. As a way of wearing "something old," an heirloom cameo pendant was stitched to the center of the simple bow. You could select a favorite charm or any piece of jewelry that has special significance to you. For a tossing garter, attach an inexpensive trinket or rhinestone button.

1   Fold the sheer ribbon in half and stitch a 1/4" (6 mm) seam across the ends; trim to 1/8" (3 mm). Then fold the ribbon in the opposite direction and stitch 1/4" (6 mm) from the first seam, encasing the raw edges. Gently press to one side.

2   Fold under 3/8" (1 cm) on one end of the satin ribbon. Beginning at the garter seam, pin the satin ribbon to the sheer ribbon, 1" (2.5 cm) below the upper edge; fold under the opposite end and abut the folded ends. Stitch along the upper and lower edges of the satin ribbon.

3   Attach a bodkin or small safety pin to one end of the elastic for inserting the elastic; attach a larger safety pin to the other end to keep it from going through. Thread the elastic through the tunnel between the ribbons.

4   Wrap the garter around your leg, and adjust the snugness of the elastic; pin. Trim the elastic to the determined length; overlap the ends and stitch them together. Stretch the garter to feed all the elastic into the tunnel and distribute the fullness evenly.

5   Make a loop with the remaining satin ribbon and the 1/8" (3 mm) ribbon; layer and hand-stitch them together. Stitch them to the satin ribbon at the front of the garter, being careful not to catch the elastic inside. Hand-stitch "something old" to the center of the loops.

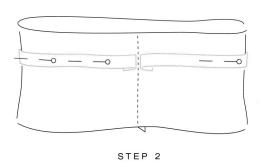

STEP 2

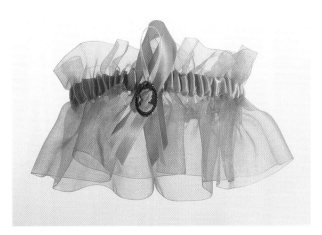

materials

Flowers

24-gauge green
paddle wire

Wire cutter

Green floral tape or
green waterproof tape

Knife

Vase of fresh tepid
water mixed
with preservative

Towel

1½" (3.8 cm) pearl-
headed pins

Wide sheer ribbon,
about 4 yd. (3.7 m)

hand-tied bouquets

FOR A FRESH-FROM-THE-GARDEN, JUST-PICKED LOOK, MAKE EUROPEAN
hand-tied bouquets for yourself and your attendants. Flowers ordered from the florist
are your best bet because they have been specially treated to last. Some varieties that work
well are suggested in the box opposite. After picking up the flowers, cut the stems 12"
to 15" (30.5 to 38 cm) in length; cut them at an angle using a sharp knife. Put the stems into
fresh, tepid water with flower preservative for a few hours. Rose stems must be placed into
water within 10 seconds of cutting. After arranging the bouquets, keep the stems in water
mixed with preservative. Dry them off and wrap them with ribbon just before the ceremony.
Because the bride will be quite busy, this is a good task to delegate.

1 If using roses, break off or cut off the thorns. Hold three flowers that will form the center of the bouquet in your secondary hand. Wrap paddle wire around the stems several times, 3" to 4" (7.5 to 10 cm) below the flower heads. Wrap snugly, but avoid cutting the stems.

2 Add individual flowers one at a time; lay the new stem across the other stems at a slight angle where the stems are held with the secondary hand. Evenly distribute the flowers around the cluster, turning the bouquet with each addition. Start each row slightly lower than the previous row. Wrap the stems occasionally with stem wire to secure.

3 Tape all the stems together three or four times with floral tape where the hand is holding the bouquet.

4 Cut the stems 4" to 5" (10 to 15 cm) below the tape, and place the bouquet in a vase of fresh, tepid water with preservative. Just before the ceremony, remove the bouquet from the water and dry with a towel.

5 Anchor the ribbon end (leaving a short tail) over the taped area by inserting a pearl-headed pin through the ribbon upward into the stems.

6 Insert a vertical row of pins upward into the stems, below the first pin. Space the pins 1" (2.5 cm) apart. Cut off the points using wire cutters if they are too long.

7 Wrap the ribbon around the back of the stems; bring it to the front, and loop it around the second pear head. Wrap the ribbon back around the stems in the opposite direction, and loop it around the third pearl head. Continue lacing ribbon in this manner to the bottom pearl head.

8 Loop the ribbon around the bottom pearl head; wrap it around the stems and loop it around the same pearl head from the opposite direction. Lace the ribbon back up the stems and loop it around the heads, as in step 7, wrapping from the opposite side.

9 Knot the ribbon ends at the top of the stems; anchor the knot with another pin, and cut the ribbon. Wrap the remaining ribbon around the knotted area, and tie it into a bow.

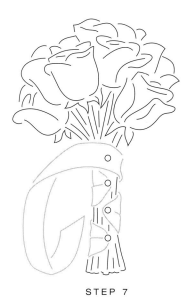

STEP 7

what flowers will work well?

Miniature or standard roses, lilies, calla lilies, miniature or standard carnations, tulips, dendrobium or cymbidium orchids, stephanotis, lily of the valley, irises, smaller varieties of chrysanthemums, freesia, ranunculus, hydrangeas

boutonnieres and corsages

FRESH BOUTONNIERES AND CORSAGES FOR THE wedding party, parents, and grandparents take a big bite out of your floral budget. You can save some money by making them yourself a day before the wedding with the help of a couple of friends. For best results, make them from flowers and greens purchased from a florist; these will come specially treated to last. Some long-lasting varieties are suggested in the box opposite. You will need to refrigerate them until they are needed, so only attempt to make as many as you can store.

Pick up the flowers on the day you intend to make the corsages and boutonnieres. Cut off 1/2" to 1" (1.3 to 2.5 cm) of the stems at an angle, using a sharp knife, not scissors. Put the stems into a vase of fresh, tepid water mixed with flower preservative for a couple of hours. Rose stems must be placed into water within 10 seconds of cutting.

In preparation for making corsages and boutonnieres, first wire and wrap the stems. Select the appropriate method, depending on whether the flower has a deep or shallow calyx under the flower head. When you are finished, mist the corsages and boutonnieres, and store them in the refrigerator in sealed plastic bags, labeled with the wearers' names. Add any ribbons to corsages after they have been removed from the bags and are dry.

Attach a corsage on the wearer's left side using a 2" (5 cm) corsage pin. Pin it to the clothing, in the natural curvature of the body, high in the shoulder area. Insert the pin through the top third of the corsage so it will not tip over, and pin through to a shoulder pad or undergarment strap for support, if possible. Attach a boutonniere using a 1 1/2" (3.8 cm) black-headed boutonniere pin. Insert the pin from the underside of the widest part of the lapel on the wearer's left side.

materials

BOUTONNIERE

Flower, greens, filler

24-gauge floral stem wires cut in half

Floral tape, 1/2" (1.3 cm) wide

Wire cutter

Boutonniere pin

CORSAGE

Flowers, greens, filler flowers

24-gauge floral stem wires, cut in half

Wire cutter

Ribbon

Corsage pin

BOUTONNIERE

1   Cut off the flower stem about 1" (2.5 cm) below the flower head. If the flower has a deep calyx (the green, cuplike base under the petals), like a rose, poke a stem wire halfway through the calyx just below the flower head. Bend both wire ends down along the stem. If the flower has a shallow calyx, like a mum, bend one end of a stem wire into a small hook and gently push the wire down through the flower and stem until the hook disappears inside the flower.

2   Wrap the calyx, stem, and stem wires together with floral tape, beginning just under the flower head. The warmth of your fingers softens the paraffin in the tape, causing it to stick to itself. Twist the flower while gently pulling the tape, so the tape spirals down around the stem and wires to the end.

3   Cut the greens stem several inches longer than the desired finished size of the boutonniere. Bend a stem wire in half; slip it over the greens stem at a point ⅔ of the way up from the bottom. Wrap the stem and wires together, using floral tape as in step 2.

4   Lay the flower over the greens, leaving some of the leaves extending above the flower head. Secure them together with one or two wraps of floral tape just under the flower head. Add small pieces of filler or more greens to the sides and bottom of the flower.

5   Wrap all the stems together as in step 2. Cut the stems about 1½" (3.8 cm) below the bottom of the flower head. Smooth the tape over the end of the wire.

CORSAGE

1   Wire and tape the flower heads, as step 1, above; wire and tape the greens stems, as in step 3. Lay the smallest flower on top of the greens, leaving some leaves extending above the flower head. Secure the top flower and greens together with one or two wraps of floral tape just under the flower head.

2   Place the next largest flower to the right of and slightly below the top flower. Wrap all stems together twice with floral tape. Place filler flowers or small greens next to the flower; secure with floral tape.

3   Repeat step 2 for the third flower, placing it slightly lower and left of the top flower. Keep adding flowers from side to side, until the desired length is reached.

4   Wrap all the stems together to the bottom. Cut the stems about 1½" (3.8 cm) below the bottom of the lowest flower head. Smooth the floral tape over the end of the wires.

Which flowers will last the longest?

FLOWERS Miniature or standard roses or carnations, pompom or daisy chrysanthemums, dendrobium orchids, alstromeria

GREENS Plumosa or leatherleaf fern, ivy, Italian ruscus

FILLERS Baby's breath, limonium, caspia, statice, wax flower, golden aster

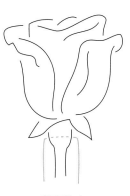

STEP 1
DEEP CALYX

STEP 1
SHALLOW CALYX

materials

20-gauge florist wire

24-gauge florist wire

Wire cutter

Floral tape

Button loops (found
in bridal department
of fabric store)

12 to 20 sturdy
long-lasting flowers

Greens and fillers

3 yd. (2.75 m) satin
ribbon, 1/4" (6 mm)
wide

Small wire-ribbon bow

Hot glue gun

hair wreath

GRACE A PRETTY FLOWER GIRL'S HEAD WITH A SWEET WREATH OF FRESH
flowers. You can make it one or two days before the wedding and store it in a misted plastic bag in the refrigerator. Just before wearing, add ribbon streamers to the back. Some
fresh flowers that will work well are suggested in the box below.

1   Wrap the 20-gauge wire three times around in a circle 1/2" (1.3 cm) larger than the
desired finished size; twist the wires together slightly. Wrap the wire circle with floral tape.

2   Hot-glue four button loops, evenly spaced, to the inside of the base. Wrap the loop ends
to the base, using floral tape. (The loops will be secured to the head with bobby pins.)

3   Wire and tape 12 to 20 flowers as on page 75, step 1; the number of flowers needed
depends on the desired fullness and the size of the flowers chosen.

4   Encircle each wired flower back with pieces of filler flower, 1 1/2" to 2" (3.8 to 5 cm)
long; join them to the taped flower stem, using one or two wraps of floral tape. Repeat
with the greens, forming tight, fan-shaped clusters.

5   Tape the first cluster to the base 1" (2.5 cm) from
the center back (halfway between two loops); hold the
flower below the head, and wrap the stem and base
together. Tape the next cluster to the base in the same
direction, overlapping the first cluster by about 1/2"
(1.3 cm), and hiding the wire base. Continue around
the base; avoid covering the button loops. Stop taping
about 1" (2.5 cm) from the first cluster. Trim off the
extra flower wires, taking care not to cut the base.

6   Just before the ceremony, cut three 1-yd. (0.95 m)
lengths of ribbon, for the streamers; fold them in half.
Hang the streamers over the center back, and glue
them in place; trim the ends to various lengths as
desired. Glue a wired ribbon bow over the streamers.

What flowers will work well?

FLOWERS Sweetheart
(miniature) or hybrid
(large, standard) roses,
miniature carnations,
and chrysanthemums
(including daisy and
other varieties)

NOVELTIES Rose hips,
hypernium berries

GREENS Italian ruscus,
plumosa fern, cedar,
smilax, ivy, variegated
ittosporum, euonymus,
eucalyptus, leatherleaf
fern, camellia

FILLERS Baby's breath,
Queen Anne's lace,
statice, limonium or
caspia

flower girl basket

FILL A BASKET WITH A SMALL arrangement of fresh flowers for your flower girl to carry down the aisle. The basket will become a keepsake for her after the flowers dry.

1   Place a plastic container or bag into the basket; secure it with floral adhesive clay. Surround the container with shredded paper or Spanish moss, if the inner container is visible.

2   Cut fresh floral foam to fit the inner container and rise about 3/4" (2 cm) above it. Soak the foam in water until it is saturated, allowing the water to soak in from the bottom and sides, but not the top, thereby preventing air pockets that could cause wilted flowers.

3   Place the floral foam into the inner container. Cut the flower stems at an angle and at the desired heights. Remove any leaves that will be covered by the floral foam.

4   Insert the flowers into the floral foam, spacing them evenly around the container and varying the heights as desired.

5   Insert the other embellishments as desired, such as ribbon loops.

materials

- Small basket with handle
- Plastic container or sturdy plastic bag to fit inside the basket
- Floral adhesive clay
- Floral foam for fresh flowers
- Shredded paper or Spanish moss (optional)
- Flowers; single variety or three different kinds
- Embellishments, such as ribbon or bead sprays

vintage ring bearer pillow

ADD NOSTALGIA AND SENTIMENT TO THE AISLE MARCH WITH A CHARMING ring bearer pillow made from an heirloom handkerchief. If you are lucky enough to have one that belonged to the groom's paternal grandmother or great grandmother, bearing his monogram, that would be ideal. Otherwise check with relatives on either side for a suitable handkerchief or select one from among the vintage linens at an antique store.

materials

Handkerchief

Spray starch (optional)

¼ yd. (0.25 m) lightweight fabric for pillow back, such as cotton batiste or silk shantung

¼ yd. (0.25 m) quilt batting

Silk ribbon in 4 and 7 mm widths in desired color

Chenille needle, size 20 or 22

Two craft wedding rings

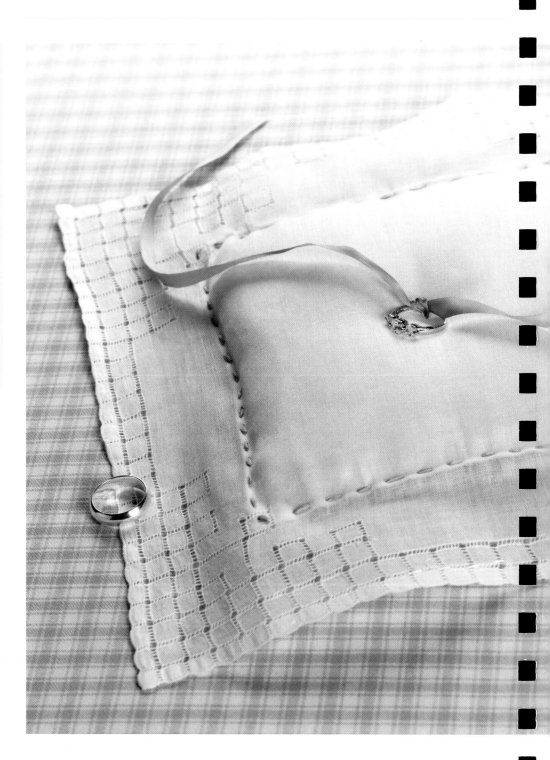

1   Press the handkerchief. Starch it if it seems limp. Determine the size of the center pillow according to the handkerchief design, leaving an outer border 1½" to 2" (3.8 to 5 cm) wide. Cut a square of lightweight fabric for the pillow back 1" (2.5 cm) larger than the determined center size. Press under ½" (1.3 cm) around the outer edges of the pillow back.

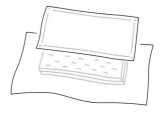

STEP 3

2   Cut two batting squares 1" (2.5 cm) smaller than the center pillow. Cut a third piece of batting 3" (7.5 cm) square. Sandwich the small batting square between the larger squares.

3   Place the handkerchief face-down; place the batting layers in the center. Place the pillow back, right side up, over the batting. Pin around the outer edges.

STEP 5

4   Cut a carrying strap of 7 mm silk ribbon 1" (2.5 cm) longer than the pillow back. Place the strap across the center of the pillow back; tuck under the ends ½" (1.3 cm), and pin them in place.

5   Thread an 18" (46 cm) length of 4 mm ribbon through the eye of the chenille needle. Pierce the center of the ribbon ¼" (6 mm) from the threaded end; pull the end of the ribbon, locking the ribbon onto the needle eye.

STEP 6

6   Fold over the free end of the ribbon ¼" (6 mm), and pierce the center of both layers with the needle. Draw the needle and ribbon through, forming a soft knot at the ribbon end.

7   Bring the needle through the fabric from the pillow back, piercing one end of the strap as you begin. Working from the pillow top, stitch the back in place using a simple running stitch. Make short, evenly spaced stitches, keeping the ribbon fairly loose so it floats on the surface. Make sure to catch the opposite end of the strap in your stitches. Remove the pins as you come to them. As you run out of ribbon, tie it off on the underside. Start another length as in steps 5 and 6. If you are adept at silk ribbon embroidery, stitch the backing to the pillow using a more decorative stitch, such as a coral stitch, stem stitch, or French knots.

8   Thread a 20" (51 cm) length of 7 mm ribbon onto the needle. From the right side, take a small stitch in the center of the pillow; don't catch the strap in the stitch. Remove the needle. Center the ribbon, and tie the rings to the pillow in a small knot. Tie the ribbon ends in a bow.

how does the ring bearer carry the pillow?

Have him hold his right hand palm up. Slip the pillow onto his fingers with the strap across the palm back and his thumb outside the strap. Place his left hand, palm up, under the right hand, covering the strap. In this position, he will carry the pillow with one corner pointing forward.

best man's ring pouch

THE BEST MAN USUALLY CARRIES THE REAL WEDDING BANDS AND HANDS them over during the ceremony. Imagine, if you will, the touching moment as the groom's right-hand man gently removes a family heirloom handkerchief from his breast pocket and unfolds the points to reveal the symbols of your everlasting love. It could be a crisply starched vintage hanky from a past generation—perhaps one that belonged to a grandmother or great grandmother. The rings can be safely tucked away in this classic fold style, sometimes called the Cagney fold.

materials

Vintage handkerchief or pocket square

Wedding bands

1   Place the handkerchief flat with points at the top, bottom, and sides. Place the rings in the center. Fold the bottom point up to the right of the top point.

2   Fold the lower left corner across to the right of the top points. Fold the lower right corner across to the left of the other points.

3   Fold the outer thirds toward the middle. Fold the bottom point, with the rings inside, upward to a depth that fits the pocket.

4   Place the handkerchief into the pocket with the folds toward the back. Adjust the four points as necessary.

STEP 1

STEP 2

STEP 3

unity candle

THE LIGHTING OF THE UNITY CANDLE FROM THE flames of two tapers signifies the joining of two lives into a new life together. As a meaningful and sentimental addition to the ritual, the bride and groom write promises to each other and seal them under a wrap around the unity candle. At a later date, perhaps their first, tenth, or twenty-fifth anniversary, they break the seal and read their promises again.

materials

Pillar candle, 3"
(7.5 cm) wide and
two matching taper
candles

Two coordinating
decorative papers, 12"
× 12" (30.5 × 30.5 cm)

Scissors with decora-
tive-edge blades

Tape, glue

Sealing wax stick

Large sealing stamp
in the groom's
last initial

Small sealing stamps
in the first initials of
the bride and groom

Candle holders

1   Cut a strip of paper for the backing 3¾" × 11" (9.5 × 28 cm). Cut a strip of paper for the outer wrap 3¼" × 12" (8.2 × 30.5 cm); round the ends.

2   Wrap the longer strip around the pillar candle and measure the overlap. Fold each strip end back half the distance of the overlap.

3   Wrap the bride's and groom's promises to each other around the candle, and tape them in place. Wrap the backing strip over the promises; tape the overlap in the back. Wrap the narrow strip over the center of the backing strip so the folded edges meet in the front. Seal the folds together with sealing wax. Stamp the groom's last initial into the wax.

4   Cut two 2½" × 3½" (6.5 × 9 cm) strips of the backing paper and two 2" × 3½" (5 × 9 cm) strips of outer paper. Wrap the strips around the tapers; tape or glue in place. Apply wax seals to the center fronts; stamp one with the bride's initial and the other with the groom's.

materials

Styrofoam cone, 12"
(30.5 cm) high

Anaglyptic wallpaper,
about 24" × 24"
(61 × 61 cm)

½ yd. (.05 m)
pregathered lace

Silk flowers and
greenery

Ribbon

Floral pins

Hot glue gun

STEP 2

STEP 4

entrance door bouquet

WELCOME YOUR GUESTS AT THE ENTRANCE TO
the ceremony or reception with a bouquet of everlasting
flowers held in a crisp white cone of richly textured
anaglyptic wallpaper. This sturdy, white, paintable wall-
covering is often used on ceilings to imitate embossed tin.
Choose flowers and ribbon to introduce the color theme
of your wedding.

1   Roll the paper around the cone. Trim to fit, overlapping
the edges in the back. Hot-glue the edges together. Trim the
paper around the top even with the flat end of the cone.

2   Secure pregathered lace around the outer edge of the cone
top, inserting floral pins through the lace into the Styrofoam.
Trim off and butt the lace ends at the back; allow the lace
to hang down over the upper edge of the cone.

3   Cut the flower stems to about 6" (15 cm); remove leaves
from the lower stems. Insert flowers into the cone, working
from the center outward. Fill in with greenery stems.

4   Wrap the ribbon around the cone as shown. Secure
at the back, using hot glue or floral pins. Secure a ribbon
loop for hanging at the back of the cone near the upper
edge, using floral pins. Insert the pins into the cone,
angling upward.

floral heart pew wreaths

materials

EACH WREATH

Two silk flower stems about 30" (76 cm) long for each wreath

Additional small silk flowers for color or texture (optional)

1 yd. (0.92 m) ribbon for each wreath

Floral wire; wire cutter

Hot glue gun

GRACE YOUR TRIP DOWN THE AISLE WITH ROMANTIC HEART-SHAPED wreaths on the pews. Though they are quick and easy to make and less expensive than real flowers, these faux-flower wreaths will transform the aisle into an enchanting walkway. Because they are designed with silk flowers, the wreaths can be made long before the wedding. For best results, select flowers that have clusters of small blossoms covering the upper third of the stems, such as the delphiniums shown here.

After the ceremony, the wreaths can be transported to the reception to dress up the bridal party chairs, gift table, or wedding cake table. Check with the site managers for their regulations on hanging decorations. Many will not allow you to use tape but may allow removable adhesive hooks that are specially made not to damage wood.

1   Bend the top of the stem down to the bottom; wrap several times with floral wire to secure. Repeat for the other flower stem. The wrapped ends will become the bottom of the heart.

2   Place one stem on top of the other. Wire them together in several places.

3   Bend the center of the top to form a heart shape. If necessary, remove leaves and reattach them across the heart top, using hot glue. Secure additional flower heads in any bare spots.

4   Form a small wire loop for hanging the wreath at the center top. Wrap ribbon around the base of the hanging loop, and tie it in a bow.

STEP 1

STEP 4

materials

8½" × 11" (21.8 × 28 cm) sheets of decorative, printable paper, one for each cone

Computer with basic publishing softwear; printer

Scissors with deckle-edge blades

Tape roller

Dried flower petals

petal cones

TRADITIONALLY, SOMETHING HAS BEEN THROWN OR BLOWN AT THE BRIDE and groom as they leave the ceremony as a symbol of wishes for a happy marriage. Rice, birdseed, and bubbles are among the top choices, though each may have its drawbacks or site restrictions for environmental or cleanup reasons. Another version of this ancient ritual is to toss fresh or dried flower petals. The petals are biodegradable and easily carried away by the wind. Simple paper cones, bearing the couple's names and wedding date, can be handed to the guests as they leave the ceremony.

1   Create a letter-size document, using publishing softwear. Center the names of the bride and groom and the wedding date, beginning about 1" (2.5 cm) from the top. Or select a favorite expression or sentiment. Use an elegant font, 14 to 18 point size; select a color, if desired. Print the papers.

2   Draw a light pencil line across each paper 3" (7.5 cm) from the bottom. Mark points 3" (7.5 cm) from the top on both sides, and draw diagonal lines from the points to the center top. Cut just inside the lines, using scissors with deckle-edge blades. Also recut the left edge with the deckle scissors.

3   Mark the center of the lower edge with a short crease. Roll the paper into a cone, with the printing on the inside and the deckled left edge on the outside; the side corners should overlap slightly. Hold the cone, with lapped corners down, against the work surface, so the deckled side edge lays flat. Apply a line of tape from a rolling dispenser along the deckled side edge. Wrap and secure the flap to the cone.

4   Prop the cones up in a basket, and fill them with dried petals.

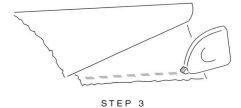

STEP 3

materials

8½" × 11" (21.8 × 28 cm) sheets of vellum, one for each lamp

Scissors

Scissors with decorative blades

Decorative paper punch in desired shape

Glue pen

Wineglass

Votive candle

Candle putty

wineglass candle lamps

NOTHING SETS THE MOOD LIKE CANDLELIGHT, ESPECIALLY CANDLELIGHT glowing though translucent paper. Inexpensive wineglasses become fancy candle lamps when topped with simple vellum shades. Use them as dramatic lighting at each place setting on the head table. Or put one on a mirror in the center of each guest table with a sprinkling of foil-wrapped candies. White, off-white, or pastel colors will allow the most light to shine through the shades.

1   Trace the lampshade pattern from page 94 onto the vellum. Cut the straight ends and inner curve using plain scissors; cut the lower curve using scissors with decorative blades.

2   Punch designs about 1" (2.5 cm) from the lower edge, spacing the designs evenly.

3   Apply a thin line of glue (a glue pen works well for this) to one straight end. Lap the other end over the glued end, forming the shade.

4   Secure a votive candle in the bottom of the wineglass, using candle putty. (This allows you to tip the wineglass for lighting.) Light the candle, and set the lampshade atop the wineglass.

grapevine chair wreaths

FOR A NATURAL, WOODSY ACCENT, MAKE THESE flower-studded grapevine wreaths for the backs of the bride's and groom's chairs. The wreaths go together so quickly, you might make one for every chair at the head table. They can be made long before the wedding, using either artificial or dried flowers. This technique also works very well for long-lasting fresh flowers, such as carnations, so you could delegate this project to someone who has more time than you on the day before your wedding.

materials

- Small grapevine wreaths
- Small artificial or dried flowers and artificial leaves or fresh miniature carnations
- Hot glue gun
- Plastic bags, toothpicks for storing fresh floral wreaths
- Ribbon, 2 to 4 yd. (1.85 to 3.7 m) per wreath, depending on the chair style and hanging method

1 Remove artificial flower heads and leaves from their stems; cut dried or fresh flower heads just below the calyx.

2 Secure the flower heads close together to the front of the wreath, using hot glue, poking the calyxes down into openings in the grapevine, if necessary. Leave a small space at the top for the ribbon. Glue leaves in scattered places under the flower heads around the inner and outer circles.

3 If using fresh carnations, mist the inside of a plastic bag. Insert several toothpicks around the wreath. Insert the wreath into the bag, and seal. Store in the refrigerator until just before the wedding.

5 Tie a long ribbon around the top of the wreath in the opening. Attach the wreath to the chair back.

RIBBON TIED TO CHAIR
BACK CORNERS

RIBBON TIED AROUND
CHAIR-BACK SUPPORTS

PINNED TO FABRIC
CHAIR COVER

wine bottle table marker

EXTEND YOUR HOSPITALITY WHILE GUIDING YOUR GUESTS TO THEIR seats with wine bottle table markers. Simply make and apply your own labels with table numbers printed on one side and your names and wedding date on the other. Display the bottles in shiny metallic bottle coasters. Depending on site restrictions and alcohol regulations, you may have to rely on servers to come around to each table, uncork the bottles, and serve the wine, especially if there are minors among your guests.

1 Create a letter-size document in landscape position, using publishing softwear. Set up guide lines dividing the document in half lengthwise and crosswise. Center a text box in each quadrant that is the same size as the opening of your picture frame rubber stamp. In a large, fancy font, type in "Table 1" in the first box, "Table 2" in the second box, etc. Center the text in the boxes. Print one or two copies as needed.

2 Change the numbers and print one or two copies. Repeat until you have labels for all the tables.

3 Create a second document. Set up guides dividing the document into 2½" (6.5 cm) squares. Create a 2½" (6.5 cm) text box in one of the guide boxes. Type the bride's and groom's names and wedding date, and center the text. Copy the text box in the remaining guide boxes. Print as many copies as you need.

4 Cut the front label sheets into four rectangles each. Stamp and emboss the picture frame stamp on each rectangle, framing the table number. Recut the labels on or just outside the outer embossed lines.

5 Cut background labels about 1" (2.5 cm) larger than the printed labels, using scissors with decorative-edge blades. Make sure they are large enough to fit over the original bottle labels. Secure the printed labels to the centers of the backgrounds, using spray adhesive. Center the new labels over the bottle labels, using spray adhesive.

6 Repeat step 5 for the printed back labels.

7 Spray terra cotta saucers with metallic paint. Allow to dry.

materials

Computer with basic publishing softwear; printer

8½" × 11" (21.8 × 28 cm) printable sheets of paper for label centers

Picture frame rubber stamp with open area about 3" × 2" (7.5 × 5 cm)

Embossing ink, embossing powder, and heat gun

Scissors

Scissors with decorative-edge blades

Decorative paper for label background

Spray adhesive

Wine bottles, perhaps a red and white wine for each table

4½" (11.5 cm) terra cotta flower pot saucer

Metallic spray paint

materials

HURRICANE RING

Mirror

One 6" (1.85 m) floral and greenery garland for every three centerpieces

Pillar candle

Glass hurricane

Ribbon, about 2 yd. (1.85 m) per centerpiece

Wire cutter

Scissors

BUD VASES

Mirror

Three bud vases; water

Three fresh roses or other flowers of choice

Three glass votives with long-burning candles

FLOWER BUCKETS

Small decorative galvanized flower bucket

Marbles or stones for weighting the bucket

Styrofoam circle or dry floral foam to fit inside bucket

Silk flower bushes, two or three varieties of different colors and textures

Wire cutter

Ribbon

floral centerpieces

FLORAL TABLE CENTERPIECES ARE ROMANTIC AND COLORFUL. THEY CAN also become quite costly if you hire a professional florist to create them for you. However, you can set the mood and save some cash by making them yourself and tapping a couple of friends to help out. One combination that always works is flowers and candlelight reflected in a mirror. Reception sites and catering companies often rent or loan square, oval, or round mirrors. Home improvement centers also carry 12" (30.5 cm) mirror tiles. You can find glass votives, candles, hurricanes, ribbon by the bolt, small bud vases, and decorative tin flower buckets at craft stores and discount centers. If you want to get some of the preparation out of the way ahead of time, use silk flowers and garlands.

HURRICANE RING

1 Cut the floral and greenery garland into 24" (61 cm) sections, using a wire cutter. Form each section into a ring by twisting the ends together.

2 Wind 2 yd. (1.85 m) of ribbon loosely around the garland, tucking the ends into the greenery. These steps can be done ahead of time and the rings stacked loosely in boxes for transport to the reception site.

3 Place the garland ring on a mirror; arrange the leaves, flowers, and ribbon. Place the pillar candle in the center of the ring and cover it with the glass hurricane.

BUD VASES AND CANDLES

1 Cut the roses to three different heights; immediately place them in water in the bud vases. Arrange the bud vases in a small triangle in the center of the mirror.

2 Place candles in the votives and arrange them in a wide triangle near the outer edge of the mirror.

FLOWER BUCKETS

1 Pour some marbles or stones into the bottom of the bucket for weight. Wedge the Styrofoam circle or dry floral foam into the bucket.

2 Cut the flower bushes into smaller sections, using a wire cutter; cut the stems to the desired heights.

3 Poke the stems into the Styrofoam, forming a pleasing bouquet.

are silk flowers cheaper than fresh flowers?

Not always, especially if you buy individual stems. You can usually get more for your money by buying silk blooming plants or bushes, which also have more leaves, and separating them into smaller sections.

what's so special about jordan almonds?

Almonds have a bittersweet taste that represents the bitterness and sweetness of life. The sugarcoating on Jordan almonds is added with the hope that the newlyweds' life will be more sweet than bitter. In Greek tradition, Jordan almonds are bundled in odd numbers as a wish that the new marriage, like odd numbers, will be indivisible.

favors

FAVORS SURE TO PLEASE EVERYONE ARE those that hold a sweet treasure, perhaps Jordan almonds, chocolate truffles, or a petit four. The treasure package itself offers you a way to express a bit of individuality while adding to your wedding theme and color scheme. While they may not be appreciated as much by the guys, little floral accents like the tiny flower-filled watering cans can really spark up a table setting. By simply applying a name tag, the favor also becomes a seating card. Favors like these can be prepared weeks ahead of time. All of the supplies can be found in craft supply stores.

materials

HEART

8½" × 11" (21.8 × 28 cm) card stock, one sheet per favor

Glue

Scissors

Slot hole punch

Desired treat

Narrow ribbon, 18" (46 cm) per favor

Threading aid, such as a bobby pin or chenille needle

Embellishments as desired

WATERING CAN

Miniature tin watering cans

Styrofoam or dry floral foam

Small-scale flowers on wired stems, usually available in bundles of individual varieties

Craft scissors or wire cutter

Metal-rimmed velum tags

Narrow ribbon

THREE-DIMENSIONAL HEART

1 Trace the pattern (page 90) onto a sheet of white paper. Draw in the fold lines. Scan the pattern. Print the pattern onto the back of the card stock. Or create one paper pattern and use it to trace the pattern onto the back side of the card stock. Cut out the favors.

2 Punch holes at the marks. Fold all of the half circles outward, toward the decorative side of the favor. Fold inward along all of the remaining lines.

3 Glue the extension flap to the inside of the adjacent straight edge. Glue half circles A and B together; glue C and D together.

4 Place the treat inside the heart. Thread 18" (46 cm) ribbon through the slots; tie in a bow. Glue other embellishments to the heart, if desired.

FLOWER-FILLED WATERING CAN

1 Wedge a chunk of Styrofoam into the can. Trim the flower stems to the desired height and insert them into the foam, creating a tiny bouquet.

2 Write the guests' names on the tags. (Lay the tags on lined paper as a guide.) Tie the tags to the can handles with ribbon.

TEA BAG FAVOR

1 Cut the card stock crosswise into 2½" × 8½" (6.5 × 21.8 cm) strips. Score the paper 3¾" (9.5 cm) from each end. Fold back on the scored lines, so the ends meet. Trim the narrow edges using scissors with decorative blades.

2 Mark off rectangles 2¼" × 2¾" (6 × 7 cm) on the coordinating paper, using light pencil lines. In the center of each rectangle, stamp the circular message. Cut the rectangles apart, using scissors with decorative blades.

3 Glue the message to the front of the favor, with the lower edge about ⅛" (3 mm) from the bottom. Punch a hole through both layers in the center of the message.

4 Place the treat into the plastic bag; place the bag inside the favor, aligning the upper edges. Punch two slots near the top, 1" (2.5 cm) apart, through the front and back of the favor and the bag.

5 Thread 12" (30.5 cm) ribbon through the slots near the top; tie in a bow.

materials

TEA BAG

8½" × 11" (21.8 × 28 cm) card stock, one for every four favors

Scissors

Table knife for scoring card stock

Coordinating decorative paper

Circular, wedding themed, rubber stamp, 2" to 2¼" (5 to 6 cm) diameter

Stamping ink

Hole punch, 1½" (3.8 cm) diameter

Scissors with decorative blades

Plastic bags, 2" × 3" (5 × 7.5 cm)

Desired treat

Slot punch

Narrow ribbon, 12" (30.5 cm) per favor

Threading aid, such as a bobby pin or chenille needle

materials

- Archival quality photo storage box
- Decorative paper to line the inside lid of the box
- Your wedding invitation
- Photo corners
- Decorative corner stickers
- Ribbons and other accents, as desired
- Decorative heart-shaped brad
- Small tassel
- Narrow ribbon for side stops
- Acid-free glue
- Craft knife
- Hot glue gun

keepsake wedding card box

AN ELEGANTLY DECORATED BOX SET ON THE GIFT TABLE KEEPS WEDDING cards neatly tucked away. While enhancing the reception decorations, this tasteful container is also the perfect way to store your wedding cards and letters long after the wedding. It is fashioned from an archival quality photo storage box and other archival quality papers and accessories, available at photo shops, stationery stores, and memory crafting stores. The lidded boxes are available in many colors and patterns, so you should have no trouble finding one that fits the color theme of your wedding.

1   Cut the corners on one long side of the box lid, using a craft knife, allowing the side to fold down flat.

2   Cut decorative paper to fit the inside of the lid. Glue the paper in place, using dots of acid-free glue. Secure your wedding invitation to the center of the paper, using photo corners; trim the message to size if necessary. Apply decorative corner stickers to the corners of the paper.

3   Decorate the box lid as desired. In the photo above, a wide satin ribbon was stretched across the lid, secured with glue to the underside of the lid ends. Three different ribbons were formed into a bow and tied to the center of the wide ribbon. Thin paper leaves, glued under the bow, echo the leaf pattern on the box.

4   Place the lid on the box. Secure the cut flap to the box, using hot glue; this will act as a hinge. (The long sides of the box become the front and back.)

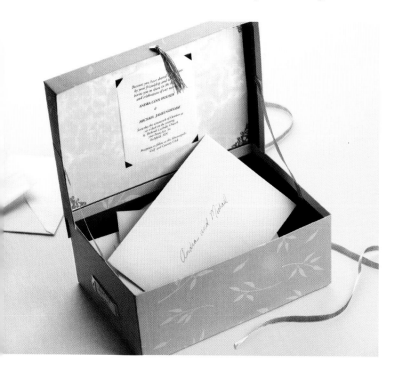

5   Secure a small tassel to the lid front, using a decorative brad; this will act as a handle for raising the lid.

6   Cut two 6" (15 cm) lengths of narrow ribbon for lid stops. Glue the ribbon ends inside the ends of the lid and box at the centers.

7   Write "Wedding Cards" on the label and slip it into the holder on one side of the box. If desired, substitute a more decorative paper for the label that comes with the box.

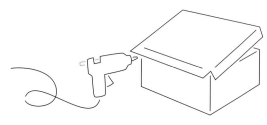

STEP 4

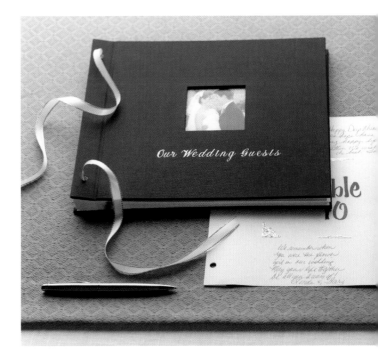

keepsake guest book

OFTEN GUEST BOOKS ARE PLACED ON A TABLE OR lectern near the entrance to the ceremony or reception which can cause a traffic jam as guests take their turns "signing in." With this guest book, individual numbered pages placed at each table assist in seating the guests and give them something to do while they await your arrival at the reception. Each guest or couple is asked to write a short memory, offer their advice, or extend their best wishes to you and your new spouse. Perhaps you could have photos taken of the guests at each table to attach to their page. When you reassemble your guest book, you will enjoy reading their messages, and you'll have a lasting, sentimental record.

Look for an archival quality album with sturdy card pages—enough for the number of tables at your wedding—that can be disassembled. The album in the photo above also has a space on the front for inserting a small photo.

1   Disassemble the album. Draw a 4" × 6" (10 × 15 cm) rectangle in the center of each page. Within the rectangle, apply letter and number stickers to label them by their table number.

2   Apply metallic letter stickers to the album cover for a title, such as "Our Wedding Guests." Add other embellishments as desired.

3   Prop the pages on small easels on their tables. Write a short note inviting your guests to write on their guest book page, and put one on each table along with a pen.

4   Reassemble the pages after the wedding. Secure the guests' photo in the center rectangle of their page over the table number. If you selected an album like the one in the photo, insert a small wedding snapshot in the space on the cover.

materials

- Archival-quality memory book/photo album

- Metallic letter stickers for the book title

- Letter and number stickers to label each page

- Additional embellishments for the album cover (optional)

- Small easels, one for each table

- Small card for instructions to place on each table

- Pens or markers for each table

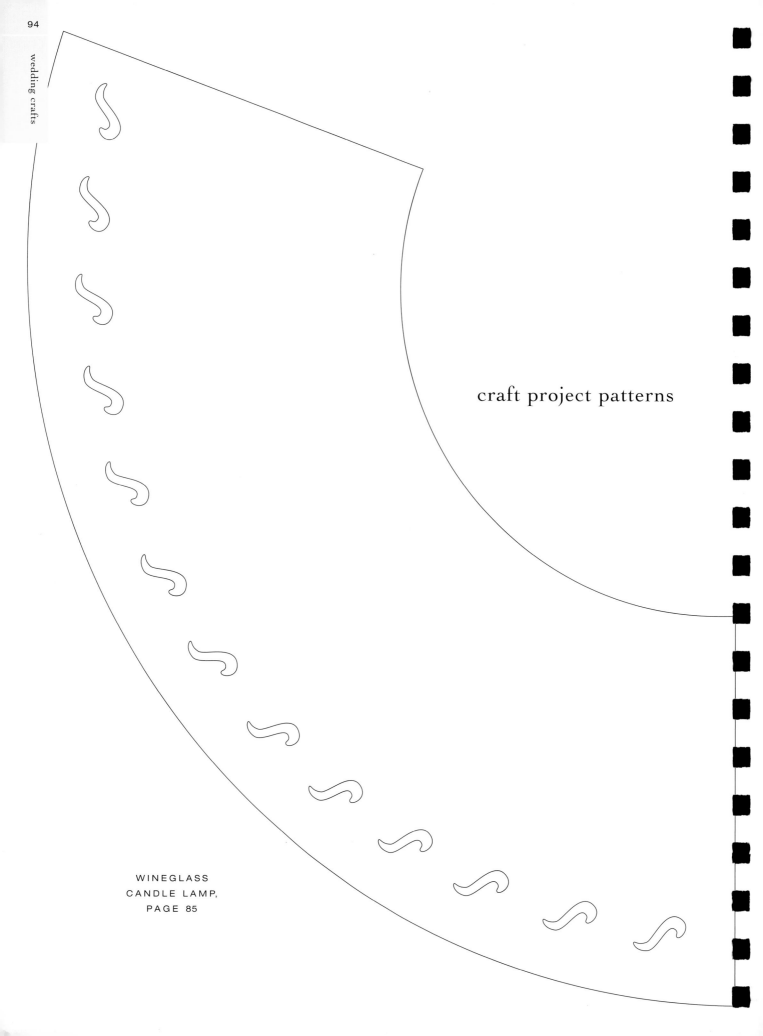

craft project patterns

WINEGLASS
CANDLE LAMP,
PAGE 85

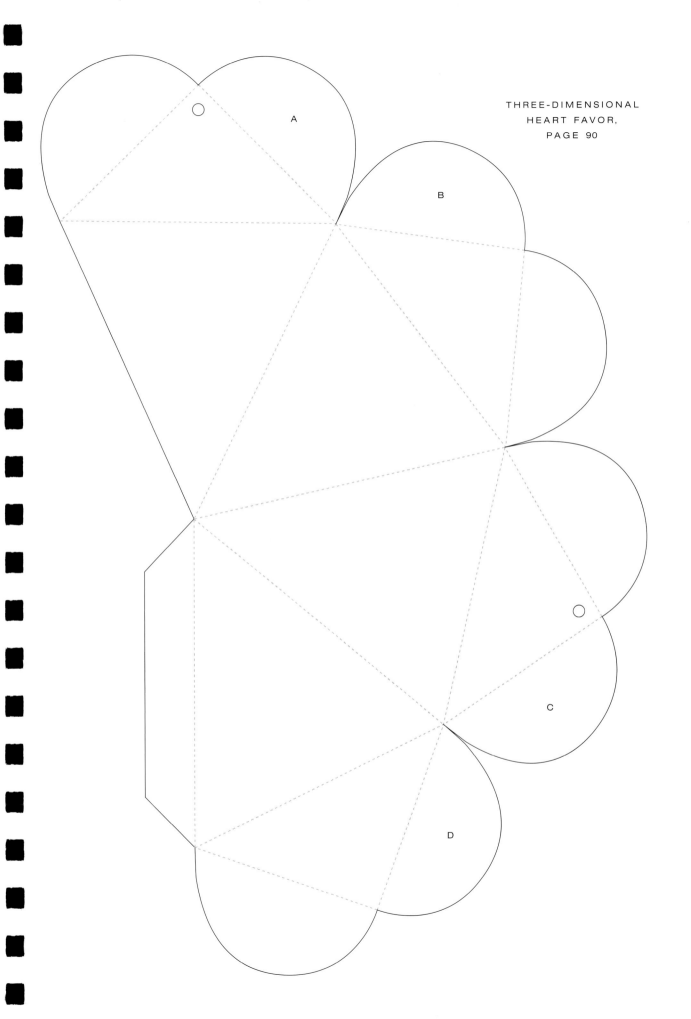

THREE-DIMENSIONAL
HEART FAVOR,
PAGE 90

A

B

C

D

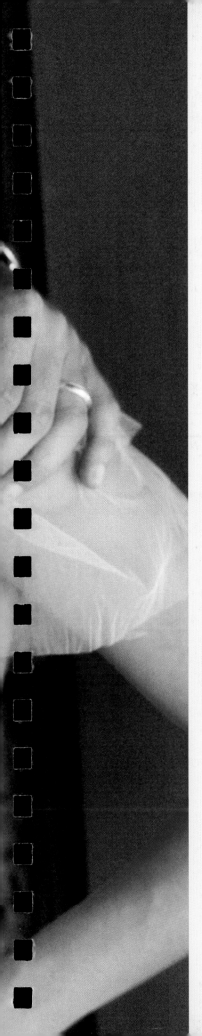

organizing tools

THE TIMELINES, INTERVIEW FORMS, LISTS, charts, and budget on the next pages will help you get organized and stay on track until you see this thing through to completion. There are places to record appointments, guest lists, seating arrangements, and important phone numbers. Make copies of the interview forms as needed. Pocket folders at the end of the book offer convenient places to store contracts, receipts, fabric swatches, and business cards. As you work through these pages, every detail you record and every completed item you check off takes you one step closer to producing and directing the wedding of your dreams. Your journey is sure to be memorable. May it also be successful!

wedding planning timeline

USE THIS GENERAL GUIDE TO HELP YOU PLAN YOUR WEDDING AND KEEP TRACK OF PROGRESS. As you make appointments, write them into your planning calendar on pages 101 to 107. As each task is accomplished, check it off and fill in specific information in the planning forms. This timeline spans twelve months, which is the ideal amount of time for planning a wedding. If you have less than a year, compress the timeline to fit your schedule, making sure that you secure ceremony and reception sites immediately and get signed contracts from professional services as soon as possible.

NINE TO TWELVE MONTHS BEFORE

☐ Announce your engagement.

☐ Set the wedding date and time.

☐ Reserve the ceremony site.

☐ Reserve the reception site.

☐ Create a wedding budget and decide how it will be divided.

☐ Decide on the style and theme of the wedding.

☐ Choose your attendants.

☐ Choose your personal attendant.

☐ Shop for your wedding gown and attendants' dresses.

☐ Shop for a photographer and/or videographer.

☐ Shop for a florist.

☐ Shop for a baker.

☐ Audition musicians or a DJ.

☐ Shop for and book a caterer, if not included with the reception site.

☐ _____

☐ _____

☐ _____

☐ _____

SIX TO NINE MONTHS BEFORE

☐ Send out save-the-date cards, if you are marrying during a busy time of year.

☐ Order your dress and discuss fitting schedule.

☐ Order or make your headpiece and veil.

☐ Order your attendants' and flower girl's dresses.

☐ Determine the size of the guest list.

☐ Compile and prioritize the guest list.

☐ Book the photographer and/or videographer.

☐ Book the musicians or DJ.

☐ Book the florist.

☐ Book the baker.

☐ Choose an officiant and schedule meetings.

☐ Select formalwear for the groom and attendants; schedule rentals and fittings.

☐ Ask groomsmen and ushers (and fathers, if they will be wearing formalwear) to get fitted.

☐ _____

☐ _____

☐ _____

☐ _____

FOUR TO SIX MONTHS BEFORE

☐ Reserve rental items needed for the ceremony and reception.

☐ Order invitations, announcements, and other stationery, if you won't be making them.

☐ If you plan to make your invitations, make a sample so you are sure you'll be pleased with the results.

☐ Shop for and order wedding bands.

☐ Help bride's mother select a dress.

☐ Inform the groom's mother of bride's mother's choice so she can select her dress.

☐ Reserve hotel rooms for out-of-town guests.

☐ Book a time for the wedding rehearsal.

☐ Start planning rehearsal dinner with the groom's parents.

☐ Book limos for the wedding party.

☐ Book your wedding night transportation.

☐ Book your wedding night accommodations.

☐ Register for gifts.

☐ Plan your honeymoon.

☐ Order your birth certificate, passport, or visa, if needed for the marriage license or honeymoon.

☐ Plan details with the caterer.

☐ Plan details with the florist.

☐ Plan details with the baker.

☐ Make appointments for your dress fittings.

☐ Have attendants make appointments for dress fittings.

☐ _____

☐ _____

☐ _____

☐ _____

TWO TO FOUR MONTHS BEFORE

☐ Have alterations completed on your gown.

☐ Select and try on all your accessories.

☐ Make accessories, such as a garter, penny pocket.

☐ Check that alterations have been completed on bridesmaids' and flower girl's dresses.

☐ Confirm details with the ceremony site manager.

☐ Confirm details with the reception site manager.

☐ Confirm details with the florist.

☐ Confirm details with the photographer and/or videographer.

☐ Confirm details with musicians or DJ.

☐ Confirm details with the caterer.

☐ Confirm details with the baker.

☐ Book salon appointments for yourself and attendants on wedding day morning.

☐ Book consultation appointment with your hairdresser to discuss your wedding day hair style.

☐ Shop for attendants' gifts.

☐ Meet with officiant to discuss ceremony details.

☐ Make your invitations if they weren't ordered.

☐ Begin addressing invitations.

☐ Help hosts schedule for showers; provide guest lists.

☐ _____

☐ _____

☐ _____

☐ _____

SIX TO EIGHT WEEKS BEFORE

☐ Make or buy ceremony and reception accents, such as unity candle, pew decorations, bride and groom chair decorations, ring bearer pillow, flower girl basket, card holder for the gift table, centerpiece components.

☐ Fine-tune rehearsal dinner details.

☐ Confirm hotel reservations for out-of-town guests.

☐ Confirm your wedding night reservations.

☐ Confirm honeymoon plans.

☐ Get blood tests if required by your state.

☐ Plan ceremony details with your officiant.

☐ Give musical and vocal selections to ceremony musicians and vocalists.

☐ Arrange to pick up your dress.

☐ Have programs printed or print them yourself.

☐ Send your announcement to the newspapers.

☐ Mail the invitations (have one weighed for accurate postage).

☐ Attend bridal showers.

☐ Write your vows, unless following the traditional script.

☐ _____

☐ _____

☐ _____

☐ _____

THREE TO SIX WEEKS BEFORE

☐ Maintain a record of invitation responses and gifts received.

☐ Write thank-you notes as early gifts arrive.

☐ Write thank-you notes for shower gifts.

☐ Take care of name changes for your driver's license, bank accounts, credit cards, and Social Security.

☐ Pick up wedding bands.

☐ Get your marriage license.

☐ Make reception favors.

☐ Give the photographer a list of must-take shots.

☐ Give a list of requests to the musicians or DJ.

☐ Arrange for delivery of cake and flowers to the reception site.

☐ Arrange a time for wedding party photography on the wedding day.

☐ Check all the contracts and make sure that you are up to date on payments.

☐ Delegate someone to attend the guest book.

☐ Delegate people to attend the gift table.

☐ Delegate people to decorate the ceremony site.

☐ Delegate people to decorate the reception site.

☐ Delegate the responsibility of transporting gifts to and from the reception.

☐ Arrange for distribution of flower petals, bubbles, or rice.

☐ Order champagne, wine, and liquor, if not included in the catering contract.

☐ Call guests who haven't responded to your invitation.

☐ Send invitations for rehearsal dinner to attendants, officiant and spouse, close family members not in the wedding, and special out-of-town guests, if you prefer.

☐ _____

☐ _____

☐ _____

☐ _____

TWO WEEKS BEFORE

☐ Work up a seating chart for the reception.

☐ Make seating cards and table markers.

☐ Address wedding announcements.

☐ Send your attendants and other wedding participants written schedules of events and duty lists for the rehearsal, wedding day, and gift opening.

☐ Give the reception site decorations, seating chart, seating cards, and favors to the people in charge of setting them up.

☐ Give the ceremony decorations to the people in charge of setting them up.

☐ Delegate someone to meet and direct the service providers at the reception site.

☐ Delegate someone to distribute flowers before the reception, if the florist will not be doing this.

☐ Arrange to have your fiancé be made beneficiary of your life insurance policy; make any necessary changes to your health insurance plans.

☐ Break in your shoes.

☐ Throw a party for your attendants; discuss accessories, make-up, hair styles, and salon appointments for the wedding.

☐ Write toasts for the rehearsal dinner and reception.

☐ Make plans for a gift-opening gathering the day after the wedding, if you wish. Invite attendants and close friends and relatives.

☐ _____

☐ _____

☐ _____

☐ _____

ONE WEEK BEFORE

☐ Give the caterer the final guest count.

☐ Give final count to restaurant or caterer for rehearsal dinner.

☐ Check in with the florist, bakery, musicians, photographer, rental centers, and transportation. Finalize pick-up or delivery and return plans.

☐ Pack for the honeymoon.

☐ Give transportation service a written schedule with pick-up times and addresses.

☐ Give service providers written schedules of reception events; assign someone to cue events (caterer, musicians, wedding coordinator, or other).

☐ Pick up your dress and veil.

☐ Pack your personal necessities for the wedding day.

☐ _____

☐ _____

☐ _____

☐ _____

REHEARSAL DAY

☐ Make any fresh floral accessories and bouquets.

☐ Pack up all the ceremony accessories and delegate someone to bring them to the site (perhaps your personal attendant).

☐ Make out final checks for other services due; arrange to have them delivered.

☐ Arrange for payment of fees or donations to ceremony participants (sexton, cantor, altar boys, etc.).

☐ Put your packed suitcases in the get-away car.

☐ Attend the rehearsal.

☐ Attend the rehearsal dinner. Make your toasts. Give gifts to your attendants.

☐ Retire early.

☐ _____

☐ _____

☐ _____

☐ _____

WEDDING DAY

☐ Eat a good breakfast.

☐ Delegate someone to put wedding announcements in the mail.

☐ Go to the salon; wear a garment that doesn't go over your head! Hair and nails should be ready at least three hours before the ceremony.

☐ Gather your dress and prepacked necessities, with the help of your personal attendant, and go to the ceremony site about two hours before the ceremony.

☐ Don't forget the marriage license.

☐ If photographs are taken before the ceremony, have the attendants arrive at least one hour early.

☐ Put your engagement ring on your right hand.

☐ Give your wedding bands to the best man and maid of honor.

☐ Give the best man the officiant's fee in a sealed envelope; ask him to give it to the officiant after the ceremony.

☐ Get hitched! Enjoy your day.

☐ _____

☐ _____

☐ _____

☐ _____

SOON AFTER THE WEDDING

☐ Host a casual gift-opening gathering.

☐ Take your gown to a reputable cleaning and storing service.

☐ Take your bridal bouquet to be preserved, if you want.

☐ Make sure all your bills have been paid.

☐ Give gifts to your parents.

☐ Finish writing thank-you notes within two months of the wedding.

☐ Freeze the top layer of your wedding cake to save it for your first anniversary.

☐ Arrange to view your photo proofs and video.

☐ _____

☐ _____

☐ _____

☐ _____

calendar

sunday	monday	tuesday	wednesday	thursday	friday	saturday

sunday	monday	tuesday	wednesday	thursday	friday	saturday

MONTH _____

sunday	monday	tuesday	wednesday	thursday	friday	saturday

MONTH _____

sunday	monday	tuesday	wednesday	thursday	friday	saturday

MONTH _____

sunday	monday	tuesday	wednesday	thursday	friday	saturday

MONTH _____

sunday	monday	tuesday	wednesday	thursday	friday	saturday

MONTH _____

sunday	monday	tuesday	wednesday	thursday	friday	saturday

MONTH _____

sunday	monday	tuesday	wednesday	thursday	friday	saturday

MONTH _____

sunday	monday	tuesday	wednesday	thursday	friday	saturday

MONTH _____

sunday	monday	tuesday	wednesday	thursday	friday	saturday

MONTH _____

sunday	monday	tuesday	wednesday	thursday	friday	saturday

NOTES

MONTH _____

sunday	monday	tuesday	wednesday	thursday	friday	saturday

NOTES

budget

USE THESE BUDGET WORKSHEETS TO HELP YOU ALLOCATE, ANTICIPATE, AND RECORD YOUR WEDDING expenses. Note that this budget does not include the honeymoon, which should be planned separately.

whom do you tip?

Budget 15% gratuities for valet services, coat check attendant, rest room attendants, wait staff, and bartenders. Check your contracts with service providers; often gratuities are already included in their fees. You are not expected to tip most professionals, including the caterer, florist, photographer, baker, or wedding consultant, unless they have performed beyond your expectations.

follow these steps

Establish a target budget total, based on the amount of money you and your families can reasonably afford to spend.

Allocate a portion of the total budget to each category. The percentages given are based on national averages. For example: If your total budget is $10,000, you can allocate $4,800 of that amount for the total reception costs. You can adjust the percentages to better suit your plans, keeping in mind that if you increase the percentage of the budget in one area, you will have to decrease it in others.

Working with one category at a time, allocate an estimated expense for each item.

Enter your fixed expenses as you go. These may include the marriage license fee, the officiant's fee, the ceremony site rental fee.

Use the estimated amounts in each category to help you make big decisions, such as how many guests to invite, how many attendants you will have, the style and location of the reception, the menu and how it will be served.

Fill in actual costs as you learn them. Record payments.

Store contracts and receipts in the folders at the back of the book.

Adjust your plans to fit your budget.

CEREMONY (5%)	BUDGET	ACTUAL	DEPOSIT	BAL. DUE	PAID
Site fee					
Officiant fee/donation					
Marriage license					
Ring bearer pillow					
Flower girl basket					
Unity candle					
Guest book and pen					
Rose petals, rice, or bubbles					
Aisle runner					
Valet service					
Rental items					
Other					

SUBTOTAL _____ _____

RECEPTION (48%)	BUDGET	ACTUAL	DEPOSIT	BAL. DUE	PAID
Site fee					
Caterer					
Wait staff and tips					
Champagne					
Liquor					
Beer					
Wine and corkage fee					
Soft drinks					
Bar service and tips					
Wedding cake					
Cake cutting fee					
Cake knife					
Table draping					
Other decorations					
Favors (each × number)					
Valet service and tip					
Parking fees					
Rental items					

SUBTOTAL _____ _____

ATTIRE (10%)	BUDGET	ACTUAL	DEPOSIT	BAL. DUE	PAID
Bridal gown					
Gown alterations					
Gloves					
Shoes					
Jewelry					
Garter					
Bride's hair and makeup					
Groom's attire					
Groom's shoes					
Groom's accessories					
Groom's hairdresser					
Spa treatments					
Other					

SUBTOTAL _____ _____

FLOWERS/DECORATIONS (10%)	BUDGET	ACTUAL	DEPOSIT	BAL. DUE	PAID
Floral delivery and setup fees					
Bride's bouquet					
Tossing bouquet					
Attendants' bouquets (ea. × no.)					
Groom/Attendants' boutonnieres (ea. × no.)					
Floral headpieces (ea. × no.)					
Flower girl basket or posy ball					
Mothers' corsages (ea. × no.)					
Fathers' boutonnieres (ea. × no.)					
Other corsages, boutonnieres (ea. × no.)					
Altar bouquets (ea. × no.)					
Pew decorations (ea. × no.)					
Reception bouquets (ea. × no.)					
Guest table centerpieces (ea. × no.)					
Head table arrangements (ea. × no.)					
Buffet table arrangements (ea. × no.)					
Cake topper					
Cake table flowers					
Cake knife flowers					
Punch table flowers					
Toasting glasses					
Other ceremony decorations					

SUBTOTAL _____ _____

MUSIC (4%)	BUDGET	ACTUAL	DEPOSIT	BAL. DUE	PAID
Ceremony musicians					
Ceremony vocalists					
Cocktail hour musicians					
Dance band or DJ					
Tips					

SUBTOTAL _____ _____

PHOTOGRAPHY (8%)	BUDGET	ACTUAL	DEPOSIT	BAL. DUE	PAID
Engagement photograph					
Bridal portrait					
Photographer's fee					
Bride and groom's album					
Parents' albums					
Additional prints (ea. × no.)					
Videographer's fee					
Additional videos (ea. × no.)					
Photo montage					
Projector and screen rental					
Other					

SUBTOTAL _____ _____

STATIONERY (4%)	BUDGET	ACTUAL	DEPOSIT	BAL. DUE	PAID
Invitations and enclosures (ea. × no.)					
Postage (ea. × no.)					
Announcements (ea. × no.)					
Postage (ea. × no.)					
Calligraphy					
Ceremony programs (ea. × no.)					
Seating cards (ea. × no.)					
Thank-you cards (ea. × no.)					
Postage (ea. × no.)					
Napkins/matchbooks (ea. × no.)					
Other					

SUBTOTAL _____ _____

WEDDING RINGS (2%)	BUDGET	ACTUAL	DEPOSIT	BAL. DUE	PAID
Bride's ring					
Groom's ring					
Engraving					

SUBTOTAL _____ _____

TRANSPORTATION/HOTEL (2%)	BUDGET	ACTUAL	DEPOSIT	BAL. DUE	PAID
Limo/car rental					
Driver tip					
Valet service and tip					
Parking fees					
Wedding-night accommodations					

SUBTOTAL _____ _____

GIFTS/PARTIES (5%)	BUDGET	ACTUAL	DEPOSIT	BAL. DUE	PAID
Attendants' gifts (ea. × no.)					
Parents' gifts					
Gifts for each other					
Bridesmaids luncheon					
Rehearsal dinner					

SUBTOTAL _____ _____

MISCELLANEOUS (2%)	BUDGET	ACTUAL	DEPOSIT	BAL. DUE	PAID
Wedding insurance					
Newspaper announcements					
Phone calls/postage related to planning					
Gown dry cleaning and preservation					
Bouquet preservation					

SUBTOTAL _____ _____

TOTAL _____ _____

ceremony site interview form

Site _____

Address _____

_____

Contact person _____

Tel. _____ Fax _____

E-mail _____

Dates and times available _____

_____

Other weddings on same day/weekend? ☐ Yes ☐ No

If yes, will site access be affected? _____

Liability insurance _____

Guest capacity _____ Handicapped-accessible? _____

Parking facilities _____

Outside officiants allowed? _____

Dressing rooms for the wedding party _____

_____

Restrictions for wedding party attire _____

Rehearsal date and time _____

_____

Decorating provisions/restrictions _____

Restrictions for tossing items after the ceremony _____

_____

Music provisions (organist, soloist) _____

_____

Outside musicians/instruments accepted? _____

_____

Wedding party photos time _____

Photography or videography restrictions _____

_____

_____

Site fee _____

Payment policy _____

Cancellation policy _____

Items/services included in fee _____

_____

_____

Items/services available for additional fee _____

_____

_____

_____

OFFICIANT INTERVIEW

Name _____

Address _____

Tel. _____ Fax _____

E-mail _____

Available on the date chosen? _____

Available for rehearsal? _____

Pre-marriage counseling (available/required/scope) _____

_____

_____

Documents to bring to first meeting _____

_____

Ceremony (general style/restrictions/allowances) _____

_____

Ceremony length _____

Vows (restrictions/allowances) _____

_____

Music (restrictions/allowances) _____

_____

Readings (restrictions/allowances) _____

_____

Sermon, homily, or speech? _____

Additional service participants (acolytes, cantor) _____

Fees _____

Attend rehearsal dinner? _____

Offer blessing or prayer? _____

Attend reception? _____

Offer blessing or prayer? _____

Fee _____

NOTES

_____

_____

_____

final ceremony plans

Site _____

Address _____

_____

Manager _____

Tel. _____ Fax _____

E-mail _____

Officiant _____ Fee _____

Tel. _____ Fax _____

E-mail _____

Date reserved _____ ☐ Confirmed

Fee _____

Deposit _____

Balance due date _____

Set-up time _____ End time _____

Dressing rooms _____

Rehearsal date and time _____

_____

Bride's vows _____

_____

_____

_____

Groom's vows _____

_____

_____

_____

Music (title, composer, vocalist, musician)

Prelude _____

_____

Processional _____

Bride's processional _____

Ceremony _____

_____

_____

Recessional _____

Postlude _____

_____

Readings (source, reader, when)

1 _____

2 _____

_____

3 _____

4 _____

5 _____

_____

Additional ceremony features (unity candle, mothers' roses, flower petals) _____

_____

_____

Decorations _____

_____

_____

_____

Photographer notes _____

_____

_____

_____

Videographer notes _____

_____

_____

Rental items _____

_____

_____

_____

Site restrictions _____

_____

_____

reception site interview form

Site _____

Address _____

_____

Contact person _____

Tel. _____ Fax _____

E-mail _____

Dates and times available _____

_____

Other events on same day/weekend? □ Yes □ No

If yes, will site access be affected? _____

Liability insurance? □ Yes □ No

Security _____

Wedding reception package options (provisions/fees) _____

_____

_____

_____

_____

_____

_____

Guest capacity _____

Handicapped-accessible? □ Yes □ No

Parking facilities _____

Valet parking available? □ Yes □ No

Coat closet/check _____ Restrooms (private/public) _____

On-site catering available/required? □ Yes □ No

(If yes, also use caterer worksheet)

Outside catering allowed? □ Yes □ No

Access to kitchen facilities (for outside caterer, baker,

beverage service) _____

Distance from kitchen to reception room _____

Liquor license _____

On-site beverage service available? □ Yes □ No

(If yes, also use beverage service worksheet)

Outside beverage service/alcohol allowed? □ Yes □ No

Policy/provisions for beverages _____

_____

_____

Table set-up (who is responsible?) _____

Extra tables available (cake, gifts, guest registry)? _____

_____

Linen choices _____

_____

_____

China/silver/crystal/choices _____

_____

Policy/provisions for decorations _____

_____

Access for decorating _____

_____

Policy/provisions for music _____

_____

Policy/provisions microphones/sound system _____

_____

Policy/provisions musical instruments _____

_____

Policy/provisions for dancing _____

_____

Policy/provisions for photography or videography _____

_____

Policy/provisions audiovisual equipment _____

_____

Additional lighting, fans, power outlets available? _____

_____

Policy/provisions trash cans and disposal _____

_____

Additional rental fees _____

_____

Manager on-site during reception _____

Reception end time _____ Overtime charges _____

Clean-up regulations _____

Site fee _____

Gratuities _____

Tax _____

Payment policy _____

Cancellation policy _____

final reception plans

Site _____

Room name _____

Address _____

_____

Manager _____

Tel. _____ Fax _____

E-mail _____

Contact person during reception _____

Tel. _____ Fax _____

E-mail _____

Date reserved _____ ☐ Confirmed

Fee _____

Deposit _____

Balance due/date _____

Cancellation policy _____

Set-up time _____ End time _____

Overtime charges _____

Guests attending _____

Parking _____

Valet service _____

Florist set-up time _____ ☐ Confirmed

Cake delivery time _____ ☐ Confirmed

Caterer access time _____ ☐ Confirmed

Bar service set-up time _____ ☐ Confirmed

Cocktails/hors d'oeuvres start time _____ End time _____

Main meal start time _____ End time _____

Open bar start time _____ End time _____

Cash bar open time _____ End time _____

Menu _____

_____

_____

_____

Service style _____

Color of table linens _____

Color of napkins _____

Place settings to include _____

_____

Centerpieces _____

Who is responsible? _____

Place cards _____

Who is responsible? _____

Favors _____

Who is responsible? _____

Decorations _____

_____

_____

Who is responsible? _____

Band/DJ set-up time _____ ☐ Confirmed

Start time _____

End time _____

Notes (electrical outlets, sound level) _____

_____

_____

_____

Photographer notes _____

_____

_____

_____

Videographer notes _____

_____

_____

_____

Rental items _____

_____

_____

_____

Site restrictions _____

_____

_____

_____

Schedule of events _____

_____

_____

_____

_____

_____

_____

_____

caterer interview form

Company name _____

Address _____

_____

Contact person _____

Tel. _____ Fax _____

E-mail _____

Person in charge during reception _____

Dates/times available _____

Other events on same day/weekend? ☐ Yes ☐ No

If yes, will service be affected? _____

Years in business _____

Catering license _____ Liquor license _____

References/photos _____

_____

_____

_____

_____

_____

_____

_____

_____

_____

_____

_____

Specialties _____

_____

_____

_____

Sample menus _____

_____

_____

_____

_____

_____

_____

_____

Tasting available? ☐ Yes ☐ No

Comments _____

_____

_____

_____

Fresh food or frozen? _____

Preparation site _____

Open to bride/groom requests? ☐ Yes ☐ No

Price range _____

Itemized or flat rate _____

Payment policy _____

Cancellation policy _____

Price includes (tables, linens, china, silver, crystal,

tax, gratuities) _____

_____

Printed prices ☐ Yes ☐ No

Special vendor rate (musicians, etc.) ☐ Yes ☐ No

Breakage insurance (included/extra) _____

Offer complete table set-up ☐ Yes ☐ No

Presentation/buffet table arrangement _____

_____

_____

_____

Choices of linens, china, silver, glassware _____

_____

_____

_____

_____

Provide wait staff? ☐ Yes ☐ No

Ratio of wait staff to guests _____

Wait staff attire _____

Provide bartending service? ☐ Yes ☐ No

Provide wedding cake? ☐ Yes ☐ No

Provide cake-cutting? ☐ Yes ☐ No

Cutting fee _____

Final count date _____

Payment policy _____

Cancellation policy _____

NOTES

_____

_____

_____

_____

_____

_____

final caterer plans

Company name _____

Address _____

Contact person _____

Tel. _____ Fax _____

E-mail _____

Person in charge during reception _____

Date reserved _____ ☐ Confirmed

Cost per guest _____

Vendor rate _____

Deposit _____

Balance due/date _____

Cancellation policy _____

Breakage policy _____

Final count date _____

Services included _____

_____

_____

_____

_____

_____

Menu _____

_____

_____

_____

_____

_____

_____

_____

_____

_____

_____

Special diet arrangements _____

_____

_____

_____

_____

_____

_____

Service style/presentation _____

_____

_____

_____

Number of wait staff _____

Attire _____

Access time to site _____ ☐ Confirmed

Responsible for table set-up?   ☐ Yes ☐ No

Tablecloth color _____

Napkin color _____

Place setting includes _____

_____

_____

_____

_____

_____

Service schedule (start time to cleanup) _____

_____

_____

_____

_____

_____

_____

Cleanup agreement _____

_____

_____

_____

_____

_____

_____

NOTES

_____

_____

_____

bakery interview form

Company name _____

Address _____

_____

Contact person _____

Tel. _____ Fax _____

E-mail _____

Person in charge of delivery and setup _____

Years in business _____

References/photos _____

_____

_____

_____

_____

_____

_____

_____

_____

Specialties _____

_____

_____

_____

_____

Tasting available? □ Yes □ No

Comments _____

_____

_____

_____

_____

Will cake be fresh-baked or frozen? _____

Choices available (flavor/filling/icing) _____

_____

_____

_____

_____

Most popular _____

Open to bride/groom requests? □ Yes □ No

Sizes/prices _____

_____

_____

Delivery charge _____

Cake cutting fee _____

Payment policy _____

Cancellation policy _____

final cake plans

Company name _____

Address _____

_____

Contact person _____

Tel. _____ Fax _____

E-mail _____

Person in charge of delivery and setup _____

Cake size _____

Style _____

_____

Flavor _____

Icing _____

Filling _____

Topper _____

Additional cakes (groom's cake, sheet cakes) _____

_____

Last date for order change _____

Delivery time _____ □ Confirmed

Cutting fee _____

Total cost _____

Deposit _____

Balance due/date _____

Cancellation policy _____

Items to be returned (pillars, stands) _____

beverage provider interview form

Company name _____

Address _____

Contact person _____

Tel. _____ Fax _____

E-mail _____

Years in business _____

Liquor license _____

Liability coverage _____

References _____

_____

_____

_____

_____

_____

_____

_____

Champagnes offered /prices _____

_____

_____

Prices on name-brand liquors vs. house brands _____

_____

Beer brands offered/prices _____

_____

_____

Wines offered/prices _____

_____

Can you supply your own?   ☐ Yes   ☐ No

Corkage fee _____

Ratio of bartenders to guests _____

Fees _____

Gratuities included?   ☐ Yes   ☐ No

Deposit required _____

Payment policy _____

Cancellation policy _____

final beverage plans

Company name _____

Address _____

_____

Contact person _____

Tel. _____ Fax _____

E-mail _____

Head bartender during reception _____

Number of bartenders _____

Hourly fees _____ Gratuity _____

Champagne servers _____ Fees _____

Access time to site for set-up _____ ☐ Confirmed

Cocktail hour start time _____ End time _____

Open bar start time _____ End time _____

Cash bar start time _____ End time _____

Champagne service time _____

Liquor choices _____

_____

_____

Beer choices _____

_____

_____

_____

_____

_____

Wine choices _____

_____

_____

_____

_____

Soft beverage choices _____

_____

_____

Total cost _____

Deposit _____

Balance due/date _____

Cancellation policy _____

florist interview form

Company name _____

Address _____

_____

Contact person _____

Tel. _____ Fax _____

E-mail _____

Other events on same day/weekend? ☐ Yes ☐ No

If yes, will service be affected? _____

Person in charge of delivery and set-up _____

Years in business _____

References/photos or actual examples _____

_____

_____

_____

_____

_____

_____

_____

_____

_____

Packages (prices/include) _____

_____

_____

_____

_____

_____

_____

_____

_____

_____

_____

_____

Provides itemized breakdown of prices? ☐ Yes ☐ No

Payment policy _____

Cancellation policy _____

Delivery and installation included? ☐ Yes ☐ No

Who is responsible for set-up, distribution? _____

_____

Florist coordinates with caterer and baker? ☐ Yes ☐ No

Bridal bouquet preservation? ☐ Yes ☐ No

Preservation cost _____

Florist's design philosophy _____

_____

_____

Flexibility _____

Has florist done weddings at your chosen sites? _____

_____

_____

Rental items available/costs (arches, potted plants, etc.)

_____

_____

_____

_____

_____

Recommendations _____

_____

_____

_____

_____

NOTES

_____

_____

_____

_____

_____

_____

_____

_____

_____

_____

_____

_____

_____

final flower plans

Company name _____

Address _____

_____

Contact person _____

Tel. _____ Fax _____

E-mail _____

Person in charge of setup _____

Tel. _____ Fax _____

E-mail _____

Date reserved _____ ☐ Confirmed

Ceremony site access time _____ ☐ Confirmed

Reception site access time _____ ☐ Confirmed

Deposit _____

Balance due/date _____

Last date to make changes _____

Cancellation policy _____

NOTES

_____

_____

PARTICIPANTS' FLOWERS	DESCRIPTION	NUMBER	PRICE
Bride's bouquet			
Bouquet for tossing			
Bridesmaids' bouquets			
Floral headpieces			
Flower girl's basket			
Groom's boutonniere			
Groomsmen's/ushers' boutonnieres			
Ring bearer's boutonniere			
Mothers' corsages			
Fathers' boutonnieres			
Other corsages and boutonnieres			

SUBTOTAL _____

CEREMONY FLOWERS	DESCRIPTION	NUMBER	PRICE

SUBTOTAL _____

RECEPTION FLOWERS	DESCRIPTION	NUMBER	PRICE

SUBTOTAL _____

TOTAL _____

photographer interview form

Company name _____

Address _____

_____

Contact person _____

Tel. _____ Fax _____

E-mail _____

Photographer in charge on wedding day _____

Dates/times available _____

_____

Other events on same day/weekend? ☐ Yes ☐ No

If yes, will service be affected? _____

Years in business _____

Wedding experience _____

References _____

_____

_____

_____

_____

_____

_____

_____

_____

After viewing examples of wedding photos, make notes of quality. Look for lighting effects, attention to detail, centered and well-framed subjects, etc. _____

_____

_____

_____

_____

_____

Bride's and groom's comfort level with photographer _____

_____

_____

_____

_____

Photographer's philosophy/style (candid, posed, traditional, photojournalistic) _____

_____

_____

Work alone or with assistant? _____

Kinds of cameras used _____

_____

Lighting and other equipment used _____

_____

Bring backup equipment? _____

Shoot in color or black and white or both? _____

Estimated number of shots/rolls of film _____

Estimated number of proofs and prints _____

Will accept and follow your must-take photo list? _____

Photographer's attire during wedding _____

Start and end times _____

Estimated time for posed group shots _____

Portrait sittings?   ☐ Yes ☐ No

Times available _____

How long are negatives kept? _____

Can negatives be purchased? _____

Digital previewing on private web site available? _____

How soon can you see proofs? _____

Viewing time allowed _____

Can you keep proofs?   ☐ Yes ☐ No

How soon can you expect a finished album? _____

Album choices _____

Parents' albums available _____

Parent album cost _____

How is cost determined? (time, number of shots) _____

Package prices available _____

Packages include _____

_____

_____

_____

_____

_____

_____

_____

Total cost estimate _____

Payment policy _____

Cancellation policy _____

videographer interview form

Company name _____

Address _____
_____

Contact person _____

Tel. _____ Fax _____

E-mail _____

Videographer in charge on wedding day _____

Dates/times available _____
_____

Other events scheduled same day? ☐ Yes ☐ No

If yes, will service be affected? _____

Years in business _____

Wedding experience _____

References _____
_____
_____
_____
_____
_____
_____
_____
_____
_____

After viewing examples of wedding videos, make notes of quality. Look for continuity, smooth transitions, centered and well-framed subjects, etc. _____
_____
_____
_____
_____
_____
_____

Bride's and groom's comfort level with videographer _____
_____
_____
_____

Videographer's philosophy/style (candid, posed, traditional, photojournalistic) _____
_____
_____
_____

Work alone or with assistant? _____

Kinds of cameras used _____
_____

Lighting and other equipment used _____
_____

Bring backup equipment? _____

Require electrical outlets? _____

Estimated number of videocassettes to be used _____

Provide wireless microphones for bride and groom? _____

Will accept and follow your must-take video list? _____

Videographer's attire during wedding _____

Start and end times _____

Overtime charges _____

Digital previewing on private web site available? _____

Edited post-production or in-camera? _____

How soon can you see a video? _____

Cost per additional cassette/CD _____

Package prices available _____

Packages include _____
_____
_____
_____
_____
_____
_____
_____
_____
_____
_____

Total cost estimate _____

Payment policy _____

Cancellation policy _____

NOTES
_____
_____
_____
_____
_____
_____
_____
_____

final photo/video plans

Photography company name _____

Address _____
_____

Contact person _____

Tel. _____ Fax _____

E-mail _____

Photographer in charge on wedding day _____

Date reserved _____ ☐ Confirmed

Total cost _____

Deposit _____

Balance due/date _____

Cancellation policy _____

Arrival time _____ ☐ Confirmed

End time _____

Given location addresses and driving directions _____

Given photo checklist _____

First viewing date _____

Web site _____

Final selection date _____

Videography company name _____

Address _____
_____

Contact person _____

Tel. _____ Fax _____

E-mail _____

Videographer in charge on wedding day _____

Date reserved _____ ☐ Confirmed

Total cost _____

Deposit _____

Balance due/date _____

Cancellation policy _____

Arrival time _____ ☐ Confirmed

End time _____

Given location addresses and driving directions _____

Given video checklist _____

First viewing date _____

Web site _____

Final selection date _____

P	V	CANDID SHOTS BEFORE CEREMONY
☐	☐	Bride getting ready
☐	☐	Bride with mother
☐	☐	Bride with father
☐	☐	Bride with both parents
☐	☐	Bride with sisters/brothers
☐	☐	Bride with maid of honor
☐	☐	Bride with bridesmaids
☐	☐	Putting on garter
☐	☐	Bride with flower girl
☐	☐	Bride with junior bridesmaids
☐	☐	Groom getting ready
☐	☐	Groom with mother
☐	☐	Groom with father
☐	☐	Groom with both parents
☐	☐	Groom with brothers/sisters
☐	☐	Groom with best man
☐	☐	Groom with groomsmen/ushers
☐	☐	Putting on boutonnieres
☐	☐	Wedding party
☐	☐	_____
☐	☐	_____
☐	☐	_____
☐	☐	_____
☐	☐	_____

P	V	POSED SHOTS BEFORE CEREMONY
☐	☐	Bride alone
☐	☐	Groom alone
☐	☐	Bride with honor attendant
☐	☐	Bride with bridesmaids
☐	☐	Bride with each attendant
☐	☐	Bride with parents
☐	☐	Groom with honor attendant
☐	☐	Groom with groomsmen
☐	☐	Groom with each attendant
☐	☐	Groom with parents
☐	☐	_____
☐	☐	_____
☐	☐	_____
☐	☐	_____
☐	☐	_____
☐	☐	_____
☐	☐	_____
☐	☐	_____
☐	☐	_____
☐	☐	_____
☐	☐	_____
☐	☐	_____
☐	☐	_____

P	V	CANDID SHOTS DURING CEREMONY
☐	☐	Overall view of site
☐	☐	Altar
☐	☐	Guests arriving
☐	☐	Guest book attendant
☐	☐	Guests signing guest book
☐	☐	Ushers escorting guests to seats
☐	☐	Groom's parents being seated
☐	☐	Bride's mother being seated
☐	☐	Groom and groomsmen at altar
☐	☐	Bridesmaids entering
☐	☐	Flower girl entering
☐	☐	Ring bearer entering
☐	☐	Father escorting bride
☐	☐	Father giving away bride
☐	☐	Groom taking bride's hand
☐	☐	Vows
☐	☐	Lighting unity candle
☐	☐	Exchanging rings
☐	☐	Officiant's pronouncement
☐	☐	First kiss as husband and wife
☐	☐	Recessional
☐	☐	Signing marriage license
☐	☐	Receiving line
☐	☐	Tossing rice/blowing bubbles
☐	☐	Bride and groom getting into limo
☐	☐	Bride and groom inside limo
☐	☐	_____
☐	☐	_____

P	V	POSED SHOTS AFTER CEREMONY
☐	☐	Bride and groom together
☐	☐	Bride with groomsmen
☐	☐	Groom with bridesmaids
☐	☐	Entire wedding party
☐	☐	Bride with her family
☐	☐	Bride with grandparents
☐	☐	Groom with his family
☐	☐	Groom with grandparents
☐	☐	Bride and groom with all parents
☐	☐	Bride and groom with all grandparents
☐	☐	Bride and groom with officiant
☐	☐	Bride and groom with both families
☐	☐	Bride and groom's hands with rings
☐	☐	Bride and groom with flower girl and ring bearer
☐	☐	_____
☐	☐	_____

P	V	CANDID SHOTS DURING RECEPTION
☐	☐	Arrival of bride and groom
☐	☐	Receiving line
☐	☐	Grand entrance
☐	☐	Head table
☐	☐	Parents' tables
☐	☐	Guests' tables
☐	☐	Buffet tables
☐	☐	Cake table
☐	☐	Best man's toast
☐	☐	Maid of honor's toast
☐	☐	Father of the bride's toast
☐	☐	Bride and groom toasting
☐	☐	Bride and groom cutting the cake
☐	☐	Feeding cake to each other
☐	☐	Bride and groom's first dance
☐	☐	Bride dancing with her father
☐	☐	Groom dancing with his mother
☐	☐	Bride dancing with father-in-law
☐	☐	Groom dancing with mother-in-law
☐	☐	Parents dancing together
☐	☐	Attendants dancing
☐	☐	Flower girl/ring bearer dancing
☐	☐	Musicians
☐	☐	Bride tossing bouquet
☐	☐	Groom removing garter
☐	☐	Groom tossing garter
☐	☐	Decorating getaway car
☐	☐	Bride and groom waving good-bye
☐	☐	_____
☐	☐	_____
☐	☐	_____
☐	☐	_____
☐	☐	_____
☐	☐	_____
☐	☐	_____
☐	☐	_____
☐	☐	_____
☐	☐	_____
☐	☐	_____
☐	☐	_____
☐	☐	_____
☐	☐	_____
☐	☐	_____
☐	☐	_____
☐	☐	_____

band/dj interview form

Company name _____

Address _____
_____

Contact person _____

Tel. _____ Fax _____

E-mail _____

Person in charge on wedding day _____

Dates/times available _____

Other events on same day/weekend? ☐ Yes ☐ No

If yes, will service be affected? _____

Years in business _____

Wedding experience _____

References _____
_____
_____
_____
_____
_____
_____
_____

For a band, how many musicians are included? _____

What instruments? _____

Music specialties _____
_____
_____

Repertoire _____
_____

For a DJ, how extensive is the music collection? _____

Work alone or with assistant? _____

For either, accommodate special requests? _____

Space requirements _____

Equipment needs _____

Serve as emcee? _____

Break schedule _____

Attire during reception _____

After auditioning, make notes of quality _____
_____
_____

Start and end times _____

Overtime rate _____

Total cost estimate _____

Payment policy _____

Cancellation policy _____

final reception music plans

Company name _____

Address _____

Contact person _____

Tel. _____ Fax _____

E-mail _____

Person in charge at reception _____

Date reserved _____ ☐ Confirmed

Total cost _____ Overtime rate _____

Deposit _____ Balance due/date _____

Cancellation policy _____

Access time to site _____ ☐ Confirmed

Start time _____ End time _____

Number of breaks _____

Play list requests _____ ☐ Confirmed
_____
_____

Cocktail hour _____
_____
_____

Dinner music _____
_____
_____

During cake cutting _____

Bride and groom's first dance _____

Bride's dance with father _____

Groom's dance with mother _____

Dance music types and special requests _____
_____
_____
_____

Last song _____

transportation interview form

Company name _____

Address _____

Contact person _____

Tel. _____ Fax _____

E-mail _____

Years in business _____

References _____

_____

_____

_____

_____

_____

Kinds/colors of vehicles available _____

_____

_____

Car sizes/capacities available _____

_____

Minimum time for contract _____

Rate structure _____

Waiting policy _____

Driver attire _____

Services included in rates (champagne) _____

_____

_____

_____

_____

_____

_____

Liability coverage _____

Gratuities included?   ☐ Yes   ☐ No

Deposit _____

Payment policy _____

Cancellation policy _____

final transportation plans

Company name _____

Address _____

Contact person _____

Tel. _____ Fax _____

E-mail _____

Start time _____

End time _____

Pick-up location(s) _____

_____

Scheduled stops _____

_____

_____

_____

_____

Number/type/color of vehicles _____

_____

_____

People per vehicle _____

Driver attire _____

Liability coverage _____

Additional amenities _____

_____

_____

_____

_____

Rate per vehicle _____

_____

Deposit _____

Balance due/date _____

Cancellation policy _____

Gratuities included?   ☐ Yes   ☐ No

attire shopping worksheet

Store name _____

Address _____

_____

Manager/contact person _____

Tel. _____ Fax _____

E-mail _____

Store hours _____

Appointments taken/necessary _____

Trunk show dates _____

DRESSES

Designers carried _____

_____

_____

_____

_____

_____

Price range _____

Allow browsing or must assist? _____

Can store order a sample dress

they don't carry?   ☐ Yes ☐ No

Extra fee _____

Shoes and undergarments provided

for trying on dresses?   ☐ Yes ☐ No

Time required for orders _____

Time for alterations _____

Alterations service provided? _____

Included in cost?   ☐ Yes ☐ No

If no, additional cost _____

Bridal gown designers and style numbers/names

for consideration _____

_____

_____

_____

Bridesmaid dress designers and style numbers/names

for consideration _____

_____

_____

Fabric samples available (for matching colors)? _____

Measurements needed by date _____

Final pressing before pickup? _____

Garment protector cover included? _____

Discounts for large orders? _____

Payment policy _____

Cancellation/refund policy _____

FORMALWEAR RENTAL

Styles/colors for consideration _____

_____

_____

_____

_____

_____

Rental fees _____

Measurements needed by date _____

Rental policy _____

Return policy _____

Cancellation policy _____

NOTES

_____

_____

_____

_____

_____

_____

_____

_____

_____

_____

_____

_____

_____

_____

_____

_____

_____

_____

_____

_____

_____

_____

_____

final attire plans

BRIDAL GOWN

Store name _____

Address _____

_____

Contact person _____

Tel. _____ Fax _____

E-mail _____

Alterations person _____

Tel. _____ Fax _____

E-mail _____

Designer/style number/name _____

_____

_____

_____

Color/size _____

Cost _____

Alterations needed _____

Date ordered _____

Deposit _____ Balance due/date _____

Pickup date/time _____

_____

Headpiece and veil style _____

Cost _____

Date ordered _____

Deposit _____ Balance due/date _____

Pickup date/time _____

☐ Shoes ☐ Stockings ☐ Bra ☐ Slip ☐ Garter ☐ Gloves

☐ Jewelry ☐ Other

BRIDESMAIDS' DRESSES

Store name _____

Address _____

_____

Contact person _____

Tel. _____ Fax _____

E-mail _____

Alterations person _____

Tel. _____ Fax _____

E-mail _____

Designer/style number/name _____

_____

_____

Color _____

Sizes _____

Cost each _____

☐ Shoes ☐ Stockings ☐ Bra ☐ Slip ☐ Garter ☐ Gloves

☐ Jewelry ☐ Other

FLOWER GIRL DRESS

Store name _____

Address _____

_____

Contact person _____

Tel. _____ Fax _____

E-mail _____

Alterations person _____

Tel. _____ Fax _____

E-mail _____

Designer/style number/name _____

_____

Color _____

Sizes _____

Cost each _____

☐ Shoes ☐ Stockings ☐ Slip ☐ Gloves ☐ Jewelry ☐ Other

GROOM'S ATTIRE

Store name _____

Address _____

_____

Contact person _____

Tel. _____ Fax _____

E-mail _____

Designer/style number/name _____

Color _____

Size _____

Rental Fee _____

☐ Shoes ☐ Socks ☐ Tie ☐ Cummerbund ☐ Vest

☐ Shirt ☐ Pocket square ☐ Cuff links ☐ Other

Rental policy _____

Return policy _____

GROOMSMEN/FATHERS/RING BEARER ATTIRE

Store name _____

Address _____

_____

Contact person _____

Tel. _____ Fax _____

E-mail _____

Designer/style number/name _____

Color _____

Sizes _____

Rental Fee _____

☐ Shoes ☐ Socks ☐ Tie ☐ Cummerbund ☐ Vest

☐ Shirt ☐ Pocket square ☐ Cuff links ☐ Other

Rental policy _____

Return policy _____

guest list

TOTAL ATTENDING _____

Name _____
Address _____
_____
Tel. _____ No. Attending ___
Wedding Gift _____ Thank-you ___
Shower Gift _____ Thank-you ___

Name _____
Address _____
_____
Tel. _____ No. Attending ___
Wedding Gift _____ Thank-you ___
Shower Gift _____ Thank-you ___

Name _____
Address _____
_____
Tel. _____ No. Attending ___
Wedding Gift _____ Thank-you ___
Shower Gift _____ Thank-you ___

Name _____
Address _____
_____
Tel. _____ No. Attending ___
Wedding Gift _____ Thank-you ___
Shower Gift _____ Thank-you ___

Name _____
Address _____
_____
Tel. _____ No. Attending ___
Wedding Gift _____ Thank-you ___
Shower Gift _____ Thank-you ___

Name _____
Address _____
_____
Tel. _____ No. Attending ___
Wedding Gift _____ Thank-you ___
Shower Gift _____ Thank-you ___

Name _____
Address _____
_____
Tel. _____ No. Attending ___
Wedding Gift _____ Thank-you ___
Shower Gift _____ Thank-you ___

Name _____
Address _____
_____
Tel. _____ No. Attending ___
Wedding Gift _____ Thank-you ___
Shower Gift _____ Thank-you ___

Name _____
Address _____
_____
Tel. _____ No. Attending ___
Wedding Gift _____ Thank-you ___
Shower Gift _____ Thank-you ___

Name _____
Address _____
_____
Tel. _____ No. Attending ___
Wedding Gift _____ Thank-you ___
Shower Gift _____ Thank-you ___

Name _____
Address _____
_____
Tel. _____ No. Attending ___
Wedding Gift _____ Thank-you ___
Shower Gift _____ Thank-you ___

Name _____
Address _____
_____
Tel. _____ No. Attending ___
Wedding Gift _____ Thank-you ___
Shower Gift _____ Thank-you ___

SUBTOTAL ___   SUBTOTAL ___

Name _____
Address _____
_____
Tel. _____ No. Attending ___
Wedding Gift _____ Thank-you ___
Shower Gift _____ Thank-you ___

Name _____
Address _____
_____
Tel. _____ No. Attending ___
Wedding Gift _____ Thank-you ___
Shower Gift _____ Thank-you ___

Name _____
Address _____
_____
Tel. _____ No. Attending ___
Wedding Gift _____ Thank-you ___
Shower Gift _____ Thank-you ___

Name _____
Address _____
_____
Tel. _____ No. Attending ___
Wedding Gift _____ Thank-you ___
Shower Gift _____ Thank-you ___

Name _____
Address _____
_____
Tel. _____ No. Attending ___
Wedding Gift _____ Thank-you ___
Shower Gift _____ Thank-you ___

Name _____
Address _____
_____
Tel. _____ No. Attending ___
Wedding Gift _____ Thank-you ___
Shower Gift _____ Thank-you ___

Name _____
Address _____
_____
Tel. _____ No. Attending ___
Wedding Gift _____ Thank-you ___
Shower Gift _____ Thank-you ___

Name _____
Address _____
_____
Tel. _____ No. Attending ___
Wedding Gift _____ Thank-you ___
Shower Gift _____ Thank-you ___

Name _____
Address _____
_____
Tel. _____ No. Attending ___
Wedding Gift _____ Thank-you ___
Shower Gift _____ Thank-you ___

Name _____
Address _____
_____
Tel. _____ No. Attending ___
Wedding Gift _____ Thank-you ___
Shower Gift _____ Thank-you ___

SUBTOTAL ___   SUBTOTAL ___

Name _____

Address _____

_____

Tel. _____ No. Attending ___

Wedding Gift _____ Thank-you ___

Shower Gift _____ Thank-you ___

Name _____

Address _____

_____

Tel. _____ No. Attending ___

Wedding Gift _____ Thank-you ___

Shower Gift _____ Thank-you ___

Name _____

Address _____

_____

Tel. _____ No. Attending ___

Wedding Gift _____ Thank-you ___

Shower Gift _____ Thank-you ___

Name _____

Address _____

_____

Tel. _____ No. Attending ___

Wedding Gift _____ Thank-you ___

Shower Gift _____ Thank-you ___

Name _____

Address _____

_____

Tel. _____ No. Attending ___

Wedding Gift _____ Thank-you ___

Shower Gift _____ Thank-you ___

Name _____

Address _____

_____

Tel. _____ No. Attending ___

Wedding Gift _____ Thank-you ___

Shower Gift _____ Thank-you ___

Name _____

Address _____

_____

Tel. _____ No. Attending ___

Wedding Gift _____ Thank-you ___

Shower Gift _____ Thank-you ___

Name _____

Address _____

_____

Tel. _____ No. Attending ___

Wedding Gift _____ Thank-you ___

Shower Gift _____ Thank-you ___

Name _____

Address _____

_____

Tel. _____ No. Attending ___

Wedding Gift _____ Thank-you ___

Shower Gift _____ Thank-you ___

Name _____

Address _____

_____

Tel. _____ No. Attending ___

Wedding Gift _____ Thank-you ___

Shower Gift _____ Thank-you ___

Name _____

Address _____

_____

Tel. _____ No. Attending ___

Wedding Gift _____ Thank-you ___

Shower Gift _____ Thank-you ___

Name _____

Address _____

_____

Tel. _____ No. Attending ___

Wedding Gift _____ Thank-you ___

Shower Gift _____ Thank-you ___

SUBTOTAL ___

SUBTOTAL ___

Name _____

Address _____

_____

Tel. _____ No. Attending ___

Wedding Gift _____ Thank-you ___

Shower Gift _____ Thank-you ___

Name _____

Address _____

_____

Tel. _____ No. Attending ___

Wedding Gift _____ Thank-you ___

Shower Gift _____ Thank-you ___

Name _____

Address _____

_____

Tel. _____ No. Attending ___

Wedding Gift _____ Thank-you ___

Shower Gift _____ Thank-you ___

Name _____

Address _____

_____

Tel. _____ No. Attending ___

Wedding Gift _____ Thank-you ___

Shower Gift _____ Thank-you ___

Name _____

Address _____

_____

Tel. _____ No. Attending ___

Wedding Gift _____ Thank-you ___

Shower Gift _____ Thank-you ___

Name _____

Address _____

_____

Tel. _____ No. Attending ___

Wedding Gift _____ Thank-you ___

Shower Gift _____ Thank-you ___

Name _____

Address _____

_____

Tel. _____ No. Attending ___

Wedding Gift _____ Thank-you ___

Shower Gift _____ Thank-you ___

SUBTOTAL ___

Name _____

Address _____

_____

Tel. _____ No. Attending ___

Wedding Gift _____ Thank-you ___

Shower Gift _____ Thank-you ___

Name _____

Address _____

_____

Tel. _____ No. Attending ___

Wedding Gift _____ Thank-you ___

Shower Gift _____ Thank-you ___

Name _____

Address _____

_____

Tel. _____ No. Attending ___

Wedding Gift _____ Thank-you ___

Shower Gift _____ Thank-you ___

Name _____

Address _____

_____

Tel. _____ No. Attending ___

Wedding Gift _____ Thank-you ___

Shower Gift _____ Thank-you ___

Name _____

Address _____

_____

Tel. _____ No. Attending ___

Wedding Gift _____ Thank-you ___

Shower Gift _____ Thank-you ___

Name _____

Address _____

_____

Tel. _____ No. Attending ___

Wedding Gift _____ Thank-you ___

Shower Gift _____ Thank-you ___

Name _____

Address _____

_____

Tel. _____ No. Attending ___

Wedding Gift _____ Thank-you ___

Shower Gift _____ Thank-you ___

SUBTOTAL ___

Name _____

Address _____

_____

Tel. _____ No. Attending ____

Wedding Gift _____ Thank-you ____

Shower Gift _____ Thank-you ____

Name _____

Address _____

_____

Tel. _____ No. Attending ____

Wedding Gift _____ Thank-you ____

Shower Gift _____ Thank-you ____

Name _____

Address _____

_____

Tel. _____ No. Attending ____

Wedding Gift _____ Thank-you ____

Shower Gift _____ Thank-you ____

Name _____

Address _____

_____

Tel. _____ No. Attending ____

Wedding Gift _____ Thank-you ____

Shower Gift _____ Thank-you ____

Name _____

Address _____

_____

Tel. _____ No. Attending ____

Wedding Gift _____ Thank-you ____

Shower Gift _____ Thank-you ____

Name _____

Address _____

_____

Tel. _____ No. Attending ____

Wedding Gift _____ Thank-you ____

Shower Gift _____ Thank-you ____

Name _____

Address _____

_____

Tel. _____ No. Attending ____

Wedding Gift _____ Thank-you ____

Shower Gift _____ Thank-you ____

SUBTOTAL ____

Name _____

Address _____

_____

Tel. _____ No. Attending ____

Wedding Gift _____ Thank-you ____

Shower Gift _____ Thank-you ____

Name _____

Address _____

_____

Tel. _____ No. Attending ____

Wedding Gift _____ Thank-you ____

Shower Gift _____ Thank-you ____

Name _____

Address _____

_____

Tel. _____ No. Attending ____

Wedding Gift _____ Thank-you ____

Shower Gift _____ Thank-you ____

Name _____

Address _____

_____

Tel. _____ No. Attending ____

Wedding Gift _____ Thank-you ____

Shower Gift _____ Thank-you ____

Name _____

Address _____

_____

Tel. _____ No. Attending ____

Wedding Gift _____ Thank-you ____

Shower Gift _____ Thank-you ____

Name _____

Address _____

_____

Tel. _____ No. Attending ____

Wedding Gift _____ Thank-you ____

Shower Gift _____ Thank-you ____

Name _____

Address _____

_____

Tel. _____ No. Attending ____

Wedding Gift _____ Thank-you ____

Shower Gift _____ Thank-you ____

SUBTOTAL ____

Name _____

Address _____

_____

Tel. _____ No. Attending ____

Wedding Gift _____ Thank-you ____

Shower Gift _____ Thank-you ____

Name _____

Address _____

_____

Tel. _____ No. Attending ____

Wedding Gift _____ Thank-you ____

Shower Gift _____ Thank-you ____

Name _____

Address _____

_____

Tel. _____ No. Attending ____

Wedding Gift _____ Thank-you ____

Shower Gift _____ Thank-you ____

Name _____

Address _____

_____

Tel. _____ No. Attending ____

Wedding Gift _____ Thank-you ____

Shower Gift _____ Thank-you ____

Name _____

Address _____

_____

Tel. _____ No. Attending ____

Wedding Gift _____ Thank-you ____

Shower Gift _____ Thank-you ____

Name _____

Address _____

_____

Tel. _____ No. Attending ____

Wedding Gift _____ Thank-you ____

Shower Gift _____ Thank-you ____

Name _____

Address _____

_____

Tel. _____ No. Attending ____

Wedding Gift _____ Thank-you ____

Shower Gift _____ Thank-you ____

SUBTOTAL ____

Name _____

Address _____

_____

Tel. _____ No. Attending ____

Wedding Gift _____ Thank-you ____

Shower Gift _____ Thank-you ____

Name _____

Address _____

_____

Tel. _____ No. Attending ____

Wedding Gift _____ Thank-you ____

Shower Gift _____ Thank-you ____

Name _____

Address _____

_____

Tel. _____ No. Attending ____

Wedding Gift _____ Thank-you ____

Shower Gift _____ Thank-you ____

Name _____

Address _____

_____

Tel. _____ No. Attending ____

Wedding Gift _____ Thank-you ____

Shower Gift _____ Thank-you ____

Name _____

Address _____

_____

Tel. _____ No. Attending ____

Wedding Gift _____ Thank-you ____

Shower Gift _____ Thank-you ____

Name _____

Address _____

_____

Tel. _____ No. Attending ____

Wedding Gift _____ Thank-you ____

Shower Gift _____ Thank-you ____

Name _____

Address _____

_____

Tel. _____ No. Attending ____

Wedding Gift _____ Thank-you ____

Shower Gift _____ Thank-you ____

SUBTOTAL ____

reception seating chart

Best Man Bride Groom Maid of Honor

HEAD TABLE

TABLE 1
_____
_____
_____
_____
_____
_____
_____
_____

TABLE 2
_____
_____
_____
_____
_____
_____
_____
_____

TABLE 3
_____
_____
_____
_____
_____
_____
_____
_____

TABLE 4
_____
_____
_____
_____
_____
_____
_____
_____

TABLE 5
_____
_____
_____
_____
_____
_____
_____
_____

TABLE 6
_____
_____
_____
_____
_____
_____
_____
_____

TABLE 7
_____
_____
_____
_____
_____
_____
_____
_____

TABLE 8
_____
_____
_____
_____
_____
_____
_____
_____

TABLE 9
_____
_____
_____
_____
_____
_____
_____
_____

TABLE 10

_____
_____
_____
_____
_____
_____
_____
_____

TABLE 11

_____
_____
_____
_____
_____
_____
_____

TABLE 12

_____
_____
_____
_____
_____
_____
_____
_____

TABLE 13

_____
_____
_____
_____
_____
_____
_____

TABLE 14

_____
_____
_____
_____
_____
_____
_____
_____

TABLE 15

_____
_____
_____
_____
_____
_____
_____

TABLE 16

_____
_____
_____
_____
_____
_____
_____
_____

TABLE 17

_____
_____
_____
_____
_____
_____
_____

TABLE 18

_____
_____
_____
_____
_____
_____
_____
_____

TABLE 19

_____
_____
_____
_____
_____
_____
_____

TABLE 20

_____
_____
_____
_____
_____
_____
_____
_____

TABLE 21

_____
_____
_____
_____
_____
_____
_____

duty list

THIS LIST INCLUDES THE POSSIBLE RESPONSIBILITIES OF YOUR ATTENDANTS AND OTHER HELPERS. Fill in the dates and times as they apply, cross out responsibilities that do not apply to your situation, and add others that may not be on the lists. Then prepare a separate list to give to each of your attendants along with your heartfelt thanks. On page 141, fill in the names of people responsible for other duties; add other responsibilities as you become aware of them. Give written lists to individuals with details of their responsibilities.

MAID OR MATRON OF HONOR	WHEN
Help the bride with wedding plans	
Lend the bride emotional support	
Help bride select a gown	
Help bride shop for attendant attire	
Get fitted for wedding attire	
Schedule own alterations appointments	
Pick up and pay for own attire	
Keep other bridesmaids informed	
Plan and host bridal shower	
Attend other bridal showers	
Record gifts at showers	
Attend bridesmaids' luncheon	
Plan bachelorette party/split the bill	
Attend rehearsal	
Attend rehearsal dinner	
Attend wedding morning breakfast	
Hair salon appointment	
Nail salon appointment	
Pose for pre-ceremony photos	
Stand beside bride at the altar	
Arrange bride's train and veil	
Hold groom's ring during the ceremony	
Hold bride's bouquet during ring exchange	
Sign the marriage license after the ceremony	
Pose for post-ceremony photos	
Ride with the wedding party to the reception	
Stand in the receiving line	
Sit at the head table	
Give the second toast	
Dance with the groom	
Dance with the best man	
Help the bride change before leaving the reception	
Be responsible for bride's gown after reception	
Attend gift opening/record gifts	
Other	

BRIDESMAIDS

	WHEN
Help the bride with wedding plans	
Lend the bride emotional support	
Help bride shop for attendant attire	
Get fitted for wedding attire	
Schedule own alterations appointments	
Pick up and pay for own attire	
Help plan bridal shower	
Attend other bridal showers	
Attend bridesmaids' luncheon	
Help plan bachelorette party/split the bill	
Attend rehearsal	
Attend rehearsal dinner	
Attend wedding morning breakfast	
Hair salon appointment	
Nail salon appointment	
Pose for pre-ceremony photos	
Stand at the altar	
Pose for post-ceremony photos	
Ride with the wedding party to the reception	
Stand in the receiving line	
Sit at the head table	
Dance with groomsman	
Dance with guests	
Other	

BRIDE'S PERSONAL ATTENDANT

	WHEN
Attend rehearsal	
Attend rehearsal dinner	
Greet and direct service providers at ceremony site	
Help the bride get dressed	
Distribute corsages, boutonnieres, and bouquets	
Attend bride and attendants during photo sessions	
Carry an emergency kit for attendants	
Provide snacks for wedding party before ceremony	
Check attendants' appearance before processional	
Move attendants' belongings from ceremony to reception	
Greet and direct service providers at reception site	
Bustle the bride's gown after ceremony	
Help bride change after reception	
Attend gift opening	
Other	

BEST MAN	WHEN
Get fitted for your wedding attire	
Pick up and pay for your wedding attire	
Plan the bachelor party/split the bill	
Attend rehearsal	
Attend rehearsal dinner	
Pose for pre-ceremony photos	
Stand beside groom at the altar	
Hold bride's ring during the ceremony	
Sign the marriage license after the ceremony	
Give the officiant his fee in a sealed envelope	
Deliver other payments as requested	
Ride with the wedding party to the reception	
Pose for post-ceremony photos	
Stand in the receiving line	
Sit at the head table	
Give the first toast	
Dance with the bride	
Dance with the maid of honor	
Drive the getaway car	
Return your wedding attire	
Return the groom's wedding attire	
Attend gift opening	
Other	

GROOMSMEN	WHEN
Get fitted for your wedding attire	
Pick up and pay for your wedding attire	
Attend bachelor party/split the bill	
Attend rehearsal	
Attend rehearsal dinner	
Pose for pre-ceremony photos	
Usher guests to their seats	
Stand at the altar	
Pose for post-ceremony photos	
Ride with the wedding party to the reception	
Stand in the receiving line	
Sit at the head table	
Dance with a bridesmaid	
Attend gift opening	
Other	

OTHERS	WHO	WHEN
Help address invitations		
Help make reception favors		
Fold programs		
Pick up guests from the airport		
Provide room and board for out-of-town attendants/guests		
Help cook and serve wedding morning breakfast		
Decorate the ceremony site		
Decorate the reception site		
Drive out-of-town guests to the ceremony and reception		
Babysit children of out-of-town guests		
Distribute rice packets or bubbles		
Clean up the ceremony site		
Attend guests at the reception until your arrival		
Move gifts from the ceremony to the reception		
Move flowers/decorations from ceremony to reception		
Be responsible for flowers after reception		
Transport gifts from the reception		
Be responsible for freezing top cake layer		
Be responsible for gift envelopes		
Be responsible for guest book		
Take bride's bouquet to be preserved		
Take bridal gown to cleaners		
Distribute final payments to service providers		
Clean up the reception site		
Mail wedding announcements		
Drive guests to the airport		
Help cook and serve food at gift opening		
Return rental items		
Other		

important contacts

Best Man _____

Address _____

_____

Tel. _____ E-mail _____

Maid of Honor _____

Address _____

_____

Tel. _____ E-mail _____

Groomsman/Usher _____

Address _____

_____

Tel. _____ E-mail _____

Bridesmaid _____

Address _____

_____

Tel. _____ E-mail _____

Groomsman/Usher _____

Address _____

_____

Tel. _____ E-mail _____

Bridesmaid _____

Address _____

_____

Tel. _____ E-mail _____

Groomsman/Usher _____

Address _____

_____

Tel. _____ E-mail _____

Bridesmaid _____

Address _____

_____

Tel. _____ E-mail _____

Groomsman/Usher _____

Address _____

_____

Tel. _____ E-mail _____

Bridesmaid _____

Address _____

_____

Tel. _____ E-mail _____

Groomsman/Usher _____

Address _____

_____

Tel. _____ E-mail _____

Bridesmaid _____

Address _____

_____

Tel. _____ E-mail _____

Groomsman/Usher _____

Address _____

_____

Tel. _____ E-mail _____

Flower Girl _____

Address _____

_____

Tel. _____ E-mail _____

Ring Bearer _____

Address _____

_____

Tel. _____ E-mail _____

Flower Girl _____

Address _____

_____

Tel. _____ E-mail _____

Ring Bearer _____

Address _____

_____

Tel. _____ E-mail _____

Personal Attendant _____

Address _____

_____

Tel. _____ E-mail _____

Bride's Mother _____

Address _____

_____

Tel. _____ E-mail _____

Bride's Father _____

Address _____

_____

Tel. _____ E-mail _____

Groom's Mother _____

Address _____

_____

Tel. _____ E-mail _____

Groom's Father _____

Address _____

_____

Tel. _____ E-mail _____

Wedding Coordinator _____

Address _____

_____

Tel. _____ E-mail _____

Ceremony Site Manager _____

Address _____

_____

Tel. _____ E-mail _____

Officiant/Clergy _____

Address _____

_____

Tel. _____ E-mail _____

Ceremony Musician _____

Address _____

_____

Tel. _____ E-mail _____

Ceremony Musician _____

Address _____

_____

Tel. _____ E-mail _____

Soloist _____

Address _____

_____

Tel. _____ E-mail _____

Soloist _____

Address _____

_____

Tel. _____ E-mail _____

Organist _____

Address _____

_____

Tel. _____ E-mail _____

Photographer _____

Address _____

_____

Tel. _____ E-mail _____

Videographer _____

Address _____

_____

Tel. _____ E-mail _____

Florist _____

Address _____

_____

Tel. _____ E-mail _____

Transportation _____

Address _____

_____

Tel. _____ E-mail _____

Rental supply _____

Address _____

_____

Tel. _____ E-mail _____

Rental Supply _____

Address _____

_____

Tel. _____ E-mail _____

Rental Supply _____

Address _____

_____

Tel. _____ E-mail _____

Reception Site Manager _____

Address _____

_____

Tel. _____ E-mail _____

Caterer _____

Address _____

_____

Tel. _____ E-mail _____

Bakery _____

Address _____

_____

Tel. _____ E-mail _____

Bartender _____

Address _____

_____

Tel. _____ E-mail _____

Reception Musician _____

Address _____

_____

Tel. _____ E-mail _____

Reception Musician _____

Address _____

_____

Tel. _____ E-mail _____

Gift Attendant _____

Address _____

_____

Tel. _____ E-mail _____

Gift Attendant _____

Address _____

_____

Tel. _____ E-mail _____

Hairdresser _____

Address _____

_____

Tel. _____ E-mail _____

Spa _____

Address _____

_____

Tel. _____ E-mail _____

Formalwear Store _____

Address _____

_____

Tel. _____ E-mail _____

Bridal Salon _____

Address _____

_____

Tel. _____ E-mail _____

Tailor/Dressmaker _____

Address _____

_____

Tel. _____ E-mail _____

Jeweler _____

Address _____

_____

Tel. _____ E-mail _____

Stationer _____

Address _____

_____

Tel. _____ E-mail _____

Rehearsal Dinner Site _____

Address _____

_____

Tel. _____ E-mail _____

Hotel _____

Address _____

_____

Tel. _____ E-mail _____

Hotel _____

Address _____

_____

Tel. _____ E-mail _____

Travel Agency _____

Address _____

_____

Tel. _____ E-mail _____

Other _____

Address _____

_____

Tel. _____ E-mail _____

Other _____

Address _____

_____

Tel. _____ E-mail _____

Other _____

Address _____

_____

Tel. _____ E-mail _____